Francesco Bartolozzi, Alexander Cozens

Principles of beauty relative to the human Head

Francesco Bartolozzi, Alexander Cozens

Principles of beauty relative to the human Head

ISBN/EAN: 9783337310967

Printed in Europe, USA, Canada, Australia, Japan

Cover: Foto ©Suzi / pixelio.de

More available books at **www.hansebooks.com**

PRINCIPLES

OF

BEAUTY,

RELATIVE TO THE

HUMAN HEAD.

By ALEXANDER COZENS.

LONDON:

Printed by JAMES DIXWELL, No. 148, in *St. Martin's Lane*, near *Charing Crofs*.

M.DCC.LXXVIII.

TO THE

K I N G.

MAY IT PLEASE YOUR MAJESTY,

WITH the warmeſt gratitude for the diſtinguiſhed honour I have received in Your royal permiſſion to dedicate the following attempt to Your Majeſty, I beg leave to lay theſe my endeavours before You.

I feel on this occaſion the moſt ſenſible pleaſure and diffidence, conſcious that I approach in Your Majeſty, the judge as well as patron of the arts.

I have the honour and happineſs of being, with the moſt profound reſpect,

YOUR MAJESTY'S

Moſt obliged, moſt faithful,

And moſt devoted ſubject and ſervant,

ALEXANDER COZENS.

L I S T

O F

S U B S C R I B E R S.

The KING.

Her Royal Highneſs the DUCHESS of CUMBERLAND.

His Serene Highneſs the MARGRAVE of BADEN.

A

THE Right Hon. Lord Apſley
Sir Charles Aſgyll, Knt.
Lady Aſgyll
Lillie Aynſcombe, Eſq;
Miſs Aynſcombe
Thomas Abdy Abdy, Eſq;
Thomas Alſton, Eſq;
Hugh Atkins, Eſq;
Mr. George Aylett
Mr. Allen

B

The Right Hon. Earl Bathurſt, Lord High Chancellor of England
The Right Hon. Earl of Beſborough
The Right Hon. Lady Beaulieu
The Right Hon. Lord Boſton
Sir George Beaumont, Bart.
The Rev. Dr. Barnard, Provoſt of Eton College
Colonel Burton
William Beckford, Eſq;
Edmund Burke, Eſq;
Oldfield Bowles, Eſq;
—— Bamfield, Eſq;
Hawkins Brown, Eſq;
Thomas Bowlby, Eſq;
George Birch, Eſq; 2 books
George Birch, Eſq;
George Birch, Eſq;
Thomas Birch, Eſq;
Miſs Birch
—— Butler, Eſq;
—— Bagnal, Eſq;
John Baſtard, Eſq;
Edmund Baſtard, Eſq;
—— Burdet, Eſq;
Maſter Barnard, of Eton
George Barret, Eſq;
—— Bacon, Eſq;
Mr. Brompton
Mr. Bretherton, 6 books
Mr. Bonner
John Bathoe, Eſq;

C

His Grace the Archbiſhop of Canterbury
The Right Hon. Counteſs of Clarendon
The Right Hon. Earl of Clanbrazil
The Right Hon. Lord Frederic Cavendiſh
The Right Hon. Lord Clive
Sir Francis Carr Clerk, Bart.
Richard Cumberland, Eſq;
Dr. Cadogan
—— Creſpin, Eſq;
Mr. Edward Coxe
Th. C. Coggan, Eſq;
The Rev. Mr. Chamberlayne
Mrs. Child
John Courtney, Eſq;
Miſs Colbourne
Miſs Cliffe
Anthony Chamier, Eſq;
Patrick George Crauſurd, Eſq;
Miſs Charlotte Collins
J. B. Cipriani, Eſq; 3 books
Mr. Coſway
Nicholas Cavanaugh, Eſq; St. Peterſburgh
John Caley, Eſq; St. Peterſburgh

D

His Grace the Duke of Devonſhire
Her Grace the Ducheſs of Devonſhire
The Right Hon. Counteſs of Denbigh, 2 books
The Lord Biſhop of Durham
The Right Hon. Lady Ducie
Mrs. Delany
The Rev. Dr. Douglaſs, Reſidentiary of St. Paul's
Charles Dunbar, Eſq;
—— Drax, Eſq;
Philip Dehany, Eſq;
Henry Duncombe, Eſq;
Charles Dumbleton, Eſq;
Richard Dalton, Eſq;
William Donaldſon, Eſq;
Mr. John Duval
The Rev. Mr. Davy
J. F. W. Deſbarres, Eſq; 2 books
—— Dickſon, Eſq;
Mr. Daniel
Mrs. Davenport
Mr. Delavaux
Mr. Davidſon

E

The Right Hon. Lady Caroline Egerton
The Right Hon. Lady Sophia Egerton
Miſs Egerton
Sir William Eaſt, Bart.
Sir James Erſkine, Bart.
George Ellis, Eſq;
The Rev. Mr. Henry Elmſal
Mr. Thomas Evans, 2 books
Miſs Ellerker
Miſs —— Ellerker
A. G. Eckardt, Eſq; at the Hague

F

The Right Hon. Earl Fitzwilliam
The Right Hon. Counteſs Fitzwilliam
The Right Hon. Lady Ann Fitzwilliam
The Right Hon. Lady Frances Fitzwilliam
The Right Hon. Lady Dorothy Fitzwilliam
The Hon. Mr. Fitzwilliam
The Right Hon. Lord de Ferrars
The Right Hon. Lady de Ferrars
Capt. French
Miſs Fleming, 2 books
Martin Fonnereau, Eſq;
Miſs Elizabeth Fountain
William Fraſer, Eſq;
Mrs. Foljambe
Mr. Fruſhard
Mrs. Fell
Mr. Flaxman

G

His Grace the Duke of Grafton
The Right Hon. Marchioneſs De Grey
The Right Hon. Marquiſs of Granby
The Hon. Mrs. Leveſon Gower
The Hon. Mr. Greville, 6 books
Miſs Grenville
Miſs Heſter Grenville
Miſs Catherine Grenville
John Grimſton, Eſq;
Robert Grimſton, Eſq;
Mrs. Grimſton
The Rev. Mr. Gilpin
The Rev. Dr. Goodenough
David Garrick, Eſq;
Francis Groſe, Eſq;
Robert Lovel Gwatkin, Eſq;
Richard Goodenough, Eſq;
The Rev. Mr. John Gooch, Rector of Benacre, Suffolk
David Godfrey, Eſq;
—— Green, Eſq;
—— Grindall, Eſq;
Mrs. Gilbert
Mr. Gardner
Mr. Gilpin

H

The Right Hon. Lord Hyde
The Hon. Lady Harriot Herbert, 2 books
Sir William Hamilton, Bart.
George Hardinge, Eſq;
Dr. Hunter
Governor Holdſworth
William Hoar, Eſq;
Gavin Hamilton, Eſq; Rome
Miſs Hartley
Samuel Hays, Eſq;
Mr. John Hunter
Miſs Iſabella Hunter
Miſs Hyde
Mr. Howard
Mr. Humphry
Mr. Hamilton
Mr. Howes
Mr. Hayward
Mr. Hardwick
Mr. Hurleſtone
Mr. Hardy

LIST of SUBSCRIBERS.

I

John Ingilby, Esq;
Mrs. Jubb
Mr. George Jeffery
Mr. Jeffery, Rome

K

The Rev. Dr. King
Richard Gervas Ker, Esq;
David Ker, Esq;
Miss Ker
Mr. Kimber

L

The Lord Bishop of Litchfield
The Right Hon. Lord Visc. Lumley
The Hon. Lady Mary Lowther, 2 books
The Rev. Mr. Langford
The Rev. Mr. Laurents, Master of Bury School
—— Leck, Esq;
Joseph Lefanu, Esq;
Miss Lockwood
Miss Lister
George Livius, Esq;
Miss Lane.
Mrs. Lambe
Robert Leigh, Esq;

M

The Right Hon. Earl of Macclesfield
The Right Hon. Earl of Morton
The Rev. Mr. Mason
Doctor Marriot
Edmund Meyrick, Esq;
James Martin, Esq; 2 books
William Mitford, Esq;
Mrs. Mountagu
Peter Michell, Esq; 7 books
Mr. Major

N

Peter Nouaille, Esq;
Captain Newton
Miss Newton
Mr. Nollekens
Mr. William Newton

O

His Highness Prince Orloff, Generalissimo of the Artillery of the Empress of Russia
Miss O'Hara

P

Her Grace the Duchess Dowager of Portland
The Right Hon. Earl of Powis, 2 books
The Right Hon. Countess of Powis, 2 books
The Right Hon. Lady Pelham
The Right Hon. Lady Polwarth
The Hon. Lady Juliana Penn
Sir John Pringle, Bart.
Sir Charles Palmer, Bart.
The Hon. Mrs. Perry
The Rev. Mr. Pennicot
The Rev. Mr. Pennick
Capt. Pratuiel, 2 books
William Mackworth Praed, jun. Esq;
—— Peters, Esq;
Thomas Poppleton, Esq;
Mrs. Jane Hanbury Pine
Mr. Pott, sen.
Mrs. Pott
Mr. Pott, jun.
Mr. Pearson
Lieut. Pierrie
Mr. John Plumptre, of Eton
Mr. Charles Plumptre
Mr. Pote, sen.
Mr. Pether
Mr. Henry Pars
Mr. Pierce

Q

His Grace the Duke of Queensbery

R

Sir Joshua Reynolds, Knt.
John Richards, Esq;
John Robinson, Esq;
Henry Raper, Esq;
Allen Ramsay, Esq;
Mr. Romney
Mr. Ryland

S

The Right Hon. Earl of Selkirk, 2 books
The Right Hon. Earl of Seaforth, 4 books
The Right Hon. the Lord Scarsdale
Sir George Saville, Bart.
Governor Singleton
—— Smelt, Esq;
Mrs. Snelling
Richard Stoneheur, Esq;
—— Smith, Esq;
James Stronge, Esq;
Hugh Seaton, Esq;
—— Stebbing, Esq;
Dr. Solander
—— Spranger, Esq;
Mr. Saunders
Mr. Stubbs

T

The Right Hon. Dowager Lady Viscountess Townshend
The Right Hon. Lady Viscountess Townshend
The Hon. John Townshend
The Hon. Thomas Townshend
Miss Townshend
Capt. Turner
Godfry Thornton, Esq;
Mr. Richard Toulmin
John Talbot, Esq;
—— Tudman, Esq;
John Thompson, Esq;
Mr. George Tierney
Mr. William Tate

V

Viscountess de Vesci
Rodolph. Valltravers, Esq; 2 books
—— Villebois, Esq;
Mrs. Vigor
Miss Maria Villettes
Mrs. Vandernan

W

The Right Hon. Earl of Warwick, 6 books
The Lord Bishop of Worcester
The Dean of Winchester
The Hon. Sir Edward Walpole, Bart.
Sir Watkin Williams Wynn, Bart.
Sir Christopher Whichcote, Bart.
The Right Hon. Alexander Wedderburn, Sollicitor General
The Hon. Mr. Walsingham
The Hon. Mrs. Walsingham
The Hon. Henry Watson
Joseph Windham, Esq;
Mrs. Weddell
Daniel Wray, Esq;
Mrs. Wray
Webb Willis, Esq;
Mrs. Wood
Mrs. Wheeler
Benjamin West, Esq;
Joseph Wilton, Esq;
Mr. Henry Watson
Mr. Wright, of Derby
Mrs. Wright, of Pall Mall
Mrs. Wright, of Newport Street
Mr. Thomas Watson

Y

Mrs. Yonge
Miss Young
Miss Yonge

PRINCIPLES

OF

BEAUTY,

RELATIVE TO THE HUMAN HEAD,

&c. &c. &c.

I DO not propoſe in this undertaking to enter philoſophically into the ſubject of beauty in general, conſequently ſhall not enquire into its exiſtence, origin, nature, or tendency. But I mean here to conſider beauty in a confined ſenſe; and in ſubmitting this work to the Public, I ſhall endeavour to ſhew by what means ſimple beauty of the human face (that is, a beautiful face unmixed with character) may be formed; as alſo that of compound beauty, which is, beauty to which ſome character is annexed---A ſyſtem, which, I flatter myſelf, may be entertaining to the lovers of art, and perhaps not unedifying to practitioners.

THE want of preciſion in our notions of beauty, has kept the world in doubt and diſpute whether or not there is ſuch a thing in exiſtence as a face of ſimple and abſolute beauty; and evident it is, that while any controverſy ſubſiſts, ſimple and abſolute beauty cannot be the ſubject of it: For while one man prefers this ſet of features, becauſe they impreſs him with an idea of modeſty; a ſecond man this air or expreſſion of countenance, becauſe it conveys a pleaſing aſſurance of benignity; a third is in raptures with beauty of a melancholy caſt, &c. it is plain theſe obſervers have mixed ſomething with the enquiry that is foreign and extraneous, namely, their own humours and predilections, and are not diſputing upon beauty itſelf, but upon the modifications of it in the ſeveral characters of modeſt, good-natured, and melancholic. In ſhort, it is not the propoſition itſelf they have under conſideration, but the corollaries branching from it: For while they continue to annex ſuch and ſuch a character to it, how can it be ſimple beauty? and ſo long as they diſpute about it in uncertainty and indeciſion, how can it be abſolute?

MY doctrine therefore is, that a ſet of features may be combined by a regular and determinate proceſs in art, producing ſimple beauty, uncharactered and unimpaſſioned. From this, as from an harmonious and ſimple piece of muſic, many variations may be derived by certain arrangements of the features, expreſſive of various characters or impreſſions of the mind, deviating indeed from the ſimple principle of beauty, but not incompatible with it.

THIS ſyſtem I propoſe to illuſtrate after the following method.

Firſt, By giving a collection of the human features, ſeparately taken, by an out-line, in profile, as large as life.

Secondly, Tables of the combinations of the features, ſelected from the aforeſaid collection, ready for the uſe of compoſing faces. The firſt table conſiſting of thoſe features which are expreſſive of ſimple beauty, and the reſt of the tables conſiſting of thoſe which are expreſſive of the various charactered beauties; as the majeſtic, the ſenſible, &c. *

Thirdly, An example of a face in profile, drawn in out-line, according to the firſt table, wherein are ſelected thoſe features which are expreſſive of ſimple beauty.

And alſo examples of faces drawn as before and according to the reſt of the tables, wherein are ſelected thoſe features which are expreſſive of the charactered beauties.

To each of the faces is applied a head-dreſs, drawn likewiſe in out-line, in the ſtyle of the antique, printed on a looſe ſheet of thin paper, through which may be ſeen the correſponding face.

IN forming theſe examples, and following the nice gradations of character conſiſtent with beauty, and void of paſſion, all the care and ability I am maſter of, have been employed. More perfect lines, or juſter expreſſion, perhaps might have been produced by more enlightened talents; therefore, I am ſenſible I muſt refer myſelf to the indulgence of the Public. However, as it is truth rather than elegance, precept rather than practice, which I wiſh to convey by my ſyſtem, provided I make that underſtood, any deficiency in reſpect of execution, will, I hope, be readily pardoned. But, as I am apprehenſive that ſome of the principles, from their novelty or from their nature, cannot but be very obſcurely communicated by words, it will be found that this defect is obviated by the

* I am deſirous here to offer a hint, that is, to make tables of features in the foregoing manner, from the moſt celebrated antique heads; and indeed it may be extended to nature itſelf, that is to ſay, to real faces. I have made a table of the features of the Venus of Medicis, as an experiment, and others may try the ſame.

examples,

examples, which being objects of ſight, are beſt adapted not only to illuſtrate but alſo to demonſtrate the abſtruſer principles.

IT remains then to ſhew by example, that there may exiſt ſuch a ſet or combination of features as conſtitutes or compoſes ſimple beauty, as before defined, without any predominant character or affection, and void of all paſſion.

THAT from this ſimple form proceed various branches of compound beauty, that is, ſimple beauty with character or affection ſuperinduced; and this I ſhall endeavour to prove from example.

IT muſt be granted, that where theſe compound or charactered beauties ſtrike the obſervers, various opinions and likings will enſue, by the preference that one obſerver will give to this character or ſtyle of beauty, another to that, &c. But theſe various opinions have no actual reference to beauty ſimply conſidered, but to the modes of it, and in which the obſerver does not decide from the eye, but from the feelings or diſpoſition of the heart.

THESE ſuperinduced characters I would be underſtood to mark ſo tenderly, as not to ſhew any degree of paſſion, nor to weaken the predominancy of beauty; proceeding in the liſt of examples in a certain gradation, from the moſt dignified and ſuperior ſort, to the moſt familiar or inferior, and confining myſelf only to female beauty, although the principles on which theſe ſpecimens are founded, are applicable to the male as well as the female human head.

IN conſidering with attention what and how many ſpecies of human character may be found to coincide with beauty, they appear to me to be ſixteen in number, and to come under one or other of the following denominations, viz.

The Majeſtic.
The Senſible, or Wiſe.
The Steady.
The Spirited.
The Haughty.
The Melancholy.
The Tender.
The Modeſt.
The Languid, or Delicate.
The Penetrating.
The Engaging.
The Good-natured.
The Timid.
The Cheerful.
The Artful.
The Innocent.

THESE, I preſume, are all the claſſes which come under the definition and limitation of charactered beauty, independent of paſſion; for I muſt again repeat, that the paſſions are by no means under my contemplation at preſent.

HERE, I apprehend, it is incumbent upon me to explain my particular meaning concerning each of the foregoing terms. The treating of them in full would be too extenſive for my preſent purpoſe, therefore I ſhall deliver my ſentiments in as conciſe a manner as poſſible. And it is alſo neceſſary to obſerve, that each of the human qualities to which the terms are applied, I mean to be a ſettled habit, not a tranſitory ſtate of mind.

BY the MAJESTIC; I mean, Dignity proceeding from a conſciouſneſs of independence.

BY the SENSIBLE, or WISE; I mean Ability, or ſtrength of reaſon.

BY the STEADY; A quality founded on reſolution of being firm, in diſtinction to tranquility.

BY the SPIRITED; The reſult of a conſtant flow of animal ſpirits.

BY the HAUGHTY; An aſſumed dignity, in contradiſtinction to the majeſtic.

BY the MELANCHOLY; Dejection proceeding from repetitions of grief.

BY the TENDER; A feeling mind, or ſenſibility.

BY the MODEST; A diffident mind.

BY the LANGUID; Delicacy of conſtitution.

BY the PENETRATING; Keenneſs, or quickneſs of perception.

BY the ENGAGING; Deſire of pleaſing.

BY the GOOD-NATURED; Sweetneſs of nature.

BY the TIMID, A habit produced from frequent apprehenſions of injury.

BY the CHEERFUL; Good-nature inclined to mirth.

BY the ARTFUL; Keenneſs, with a little ſelf-gratification.

BY the INNOCENT; A character void of harm, and alſo that has no ſuſpicion of harm.

IT

IT may be obſerved in the human face that, in general, Nature has aſſigned a ſeat for each of the following effects, viz. beauty, expreſſion, and dignity; and I preſume, that the firſt is placed in the forehead and noſe; the ſecond in the eyes and mouth; the third in the chin, and ſometimes in the forehead and noſe conjointly; examples of theſe may be pointed out, eſpecially amongſt the antique heads.

HERE may be ventured a conjecture, that what is called the ſtraight, Grecian noſe, and its being ſaid to be the ſtandard of beautiful taſte in that reſpect, proceeds from an inaccuracy of obſervation. The author's idea of the ſtate of the caſe is this. That of the gently curved lines of beauty, as in the noſe, forehead, &c. thoſe are the moſt beautiful which deviate leaſt from the ſtraight line. The ancients have executed that ſpecies of lines which I call gently curved, in forming the feature in queſtion (the noſe) in ſuch a manner, as to cauſe the appearance of theſe lines to deviate ſo little from the ſtraight line, that, to the generality of obſervers, they all ſeem ſtraight, the nice variations not being attended to; and from this it is probable, that the general opinion has ariſen, of the Grecian noſe being ſtraight, and therefore the ſtandard of taſte as to that feature.

FROM what has been ſaid, in general, I think it may be eſtabliſhed as a principle, "That beauty and character of the face conſiſt in form and colour; but that paſſion "and grace depend upon action." The latter part of the propoſition is ſo underſtood by Milton, when he ſays,

> "Grace was in all her *Steps*, heav'n in her eye;
> "In all her *Geſtures* dignity and *Love*."

And Homer, in his deſcriptions of Apollo does not fail to draw him in action, as expreſſive of his divine grace; whilſt Jupiter, conformably to the majeſty of his character, is repreſented more ſedentary and quieſcent.

ALTHOUGH the variety that is ſeen in beautiful faces is very evident, yet we are not able immediately to gueſs the particular diſtinction perhaps of any one of them, ſo as to give it a name. This is cauſed by the delicate connection of character with beauty, beauty communicating a certain degree of ſimilitude to them all; which renders the diſtinctions ſo nice and latent. If this effect is viſible throughout the examples in this work, then I hope it may be allowed that I have copied nature in that reſpect.

MANY thouſands of different combinations of the features may be made, among which there will be many void of character and beauty, but exhibiting certain ideas of mixed countenance, (as the ſame occur to us daily in common life); yet others may expreſs both beauty and character, and probably to a greater degree of truth than thoſe which are made out in theſe examples. The trial of this is left to the Public at large. With a view to this trial, the present work is constructed in such a manner that any person inclined to study it, may amuse himself in forming new ideas of heads by combining the features differently.

THE method I made use of was first to settle or determine the idea of the simple beauty, by selecting the features out of the collection which I thought would produce that idea. After this, I traced these selected features one after another in their proper places (beginning with the forehead), thro' a thin or transparent sheet of paper. And thus the out-line of the simple beauty being compleated, I made use of it as a plan or ground-work for forming all the subsequent charactered beauties. In executing each of these, I placed a sheet of very thin paper on this out-line of simple beauty, and altered the features therein to those in the collection which appeared to be conducive to the character or species of beauty in contemplation. I was convinced also, that the expressions in the faces might be considerably augmented by suitable dresses of the hair. I have therefore composed as many of them as there are faces, interleaving them where I presumed they were best adapted, proposing that they should be applied to or laid over the faces so as to produce the most proper effect. For this purpose they are printed on transparent paper, and intended not to be bound in the book, in order to give an opportunity of moving them at pleasure on any one face, and likewise of applying them to any of the rest of the faces.

I BEG leave to observe, that I have purposely rejected every collateral assistance that might recommend the drawings of the examples to a common eye, such as shading, softness, free-drawing, &c. This is adopted, that the merit of these examples shall stand upon the simple foundation of out-line alone; and even these out-lines I have chosen to draw in such a manner as to approach to something like mathematical precision. This I thought was bringing my system to the severest trial, of which I am very desirous. But I warmly wish, that some sculptor of ability would think it worth his while to render a set of examples of the simple and charactered beauties perfect, in models of clay, or executed in marble, that may be relied upon as standards of beauty to future ages.

IN considering the subject I was led to make the following observations, which I presume to offer to the Public.

SIMPLE beauty of the human face is one and the same at all times and in all places, and is void of any predominant mental character. It proceeds from certain properties in the object, peculiarly adapted to raise that idea, the investigation of which I do not undertake. Thus, were all womankind of the simple beauty, they would resemble each other. This extreme simplicity of countenance we may suppose to be visible in the face of Eve, whose vacant mind is described in the following lines of Milton in his Paradise Lost, and are here given with a small variation.

That

That day I oft remember, when from ſleep
I firſt awak'd, and found myſelf repos'd
Under a ſhade on flowers, unknowing where
And what I was, whence thither brought, and why.

AS to other characteriſtics of ſimple beauty, they are juſtly marked in Adam's deſcription of Eve at her creation, in the ſame poem.

" Under his forming hand a creature grew,
" Manlike, but different ſex, ſo lovely fair,
" That what ſeem'd fair in all the world ſeem'd now
" Mean, or in her ſumm'd up, in her combin'd
" And in her looks," ——

SIMPLE beauty may be compared to pure, elemental water, and character is to beauty as flavour, ſcent, and colour are to water, which, by the addition of theſe ſeveral infuſions, will be termed ſweet, or ſour, or ſcented, or red, yellow, &c. i. e. ſpecies or ſorts of water. For the addition of character to beauty gives the latter a diſtinguiſhing quality, producing all the different kinds of charactered beauties, each equally pleaſing as to the effect upon the different taſtes of mankind, but inferior to the firſt or ſimple beauty, in regard to purity of beauty. Thus, as I ſuppoſe that there is ſuch a thing as elemental water, ſo I preſume that there is elemental beauty, independent of taſte or prepoſſeſſion, but capable of being blended with other qualities. As water may be mixt with wine, milk, &c. in the ſame glaſs; ſo beauty with the expreſſion of majeſty, or beauty with ſenſe, &c. may be combined in the ſame face: The infuſion gives flavour or expreſſion to the inſipid element; and it may be obſerved, that ſome characters will unite more intimately with beauty than others, as it is eaſy to conceive that the ſteady, the artful, &c. accord leſs with beauty than the modeſt, the good-natured, &c. Hence it ſhould ſeem that ſimple beauty is pure, becauſe it has no character, and charactered beauty is in ſome degree impure, if it may be ſo expreſſed, becauſe its beauty is not ſimple and unmixed.

THEREFORE, according to theſe obſervations, beauty, in one ſenſe, is invariable, as in the ſimple; in another ſenſe it is varied, as in the charactered. And further, it may be probable, it is ordained, that among mankind there ſhall be certain ſpecies of taſte or fancy adapted to the various ſpecies of charactered beauty; (on this footing may be placed all the different local taſtes of beauty, as the Chineſe, the Ethiopian, the Hottentot, &c. although the extravagance of ſome of them appear to Europeans to deviate from ſimple beauty into deformity)---And likewiſe, that there are ſome men who poſſeſs a power of diſcernment which enables them to perceive ſimple or unmixed beauty. In other words, that there are claſſes of men who are attached to each of the charactered beauties reſpectively, and theſe will not be ſtruck with the appearance of ſimple beauty; and that there is a claſs of men whoſe nice diſcernment and taſte inclines them to admire the ſimple beauty, and this claſs will think the charactered beauties imperfect. I am inclined to believe that ſimple beauty, from its inſipidity, eſcapes the notice of mankind, they, from their avocations, paſſions, and habits or cuſtoms, being ill-diſpoſed to diſcern, and when diſcerned, the impreſſion is ſoon obliterated by the forementioned prepoſſeſſions, as thoſe who have inured themſelves to drink ſtronger liquors, will not be made to reliſh the purity of water. Therefore it may be preſumed, thoſe perſons are the moſt capable of perceiving ſimple beauty, who are moſt free from the hurry of avocations, influence of paſſions, and inveteracy of habit or cuſtom.

THE effect of ſimple beauty on the ſpectator is, admiration mixed with pleaſure, affording amuſement in beholding it; the powers of the charactered beauties raiſe other emotions alſo, tending to intereſt the paſſions. Here an obſervation has occurred to me concerning ſimple beauty of the human face, that it poſſeſſes this ſingular property, it will amuſe the curious obſerver, by making him fancy or imagine that this face has a latent capacity for (or with the addition of habit may aſſume hereafter) that character with which his taſte is in alliance, and this raiſes in him a certain ſelf-approbation for having the penetration of finding it out. Another curious obſerver may be amuſed in the ſame manner with the ſame face, fancying he has diſcovered in it a capacity towards a certain character perfectly agreeable to his taſte, totally different from that of the other. And thus, ſimple beauty may afford a fund of this kind for the amuſement of ſpectators perhaps of every taſte, or ſome few excepted.

SIMPLE beauty as exiſting in nature, which I ſuppoſe it does, cannot be made uſe of as a ſtandard to proceed from in any work of art, becauſe perhaps it is impoſſible for the human faculties to diſcern where it can be found pure. The example here given of ſimple beauty is deſigned only as a ſubſtitute for that which is ſo difficult to be found in nature; yet frequent eſſays towards it by perſons of refined intellects, may bring ſome future ſpecimens or examples nearer to the point of pure and ſimple beauty.

IN regard to a ſuppoſition that the application of this work to practice, will ſhackle or cramp genius; it may be anſwered, that notwithſtanding the mechanic principles upon which this ſyſtem is built, it will not follow, that a painter or ſtatuary, by adhering to them only, muſt neceſſarily be enabled to produce a repreſentation of beauty or of character; but he may be aſſiſted by them; for theſe repreſentations depend not only upon the beautiful forms, or the different variations of the features, but likewiſe on the aſſortment, poſition, proportion, and compariſons of them, the adjuſtment of which belongs to the province of genius. Therefore, this circumſtance affords the greateſt latitude to the taſte and judgment of the compoſer, whilſt principles and rules have it not in their power to circumſcribe the bounds of genius.

BEAUTY confidered in comparifon with deformity admits of a gradation, for a fmall deviation from the fimple or pure beauty is a degree of deformity, as a fmall deviation from light is a degree of darknefs. But between fimple beauty and extreme deformity a certain point is fuppofed; the deviations from pure beauty to this point are ftyled the different degrees of beauty, and all the degrees from thence to extreme deformity are ftyled degrees of deformity. But there are more degrees of deformity than of beauty, as there are a greater number of irregular forms than regular. For this reafon perhaps it would be more difficult to find a ftandard for extreme deformity, than for fimple beauty.

IN the courfe of my contemplating the various kinds of beautiful faces, and frequently reviewing the examples of them in this work, an effect or appearance in the human countenance has prefented itfelf to me, which, perhaps, is new, and may be ufeful in the art of painting. I therefore am induced to offer this occurrence in the light it ftrikes me, and to fubmit the truth and accuracy of the propofition to the confideration of the curious, who will decide it at laft whether it be any thing more than conjecture; it is this, Firft, that the face of fimple beauty feems to exhibit fome faint appearance of all the mental characters, except the fpirited, the haughty, and the artful, as light, according to Sir Ifaac Newton, contains all the prifmatic colours. Secondly, that in all the faces of charactered beauty may be feen a fmall degree of each other. I hope the unavoidable obfcurity of this will be cleared up in the following arrangement.

IN the SIMPLE BEAUTY may be feen a fmall degree of the Majeftic, Senfible, Steady, Melancholic, Tender, Modeft, Languid, Penetrating, Engaging, Good-natured, Timid, Chearful, Innocent.

IN the MAJESTIC may be feen a fmall degree of the Senfible, Steady, Spirited, Haughty, Penetrating, Good-natured.

IN the SENSIBLE are the Majeftic, Steady, Penetrating.

IN the STEADY,---the Majeftic, Senfible, Spirited, Haughty, Penetrating.

IN the SPIRITED,---the Majeftic, Senfible, Penetrating.

IN the HAUGHTY,---the Majeftic, Senfible, Steady.

IN the MELANCHOLIC,---the Senfible, Modeft, Languid.

IN the TENDER,---the Senfible, Melancholic, Modeft, Languid, Penetrating, Good-natured, Timid, Innocent.

IN the MODEST,—the Senſible, Good-natured, Timid, Innocent.

IN the LANGUID,---the Senſible, Modeſt, Timid.

IN the PENETRATING,---the Senſible, Spirited.

IN the ENGAGING,---the Senſible, Spirited, Penetrating, Good-natured, Artful.

IN the GOOD-NATURED,---the Senſible, Chearful, Innocent.

IN the TIMID,---the Senſible, Tender, Modeſt, Penetrating.

IN the CHEARFUL,---the Spirited, Good-natured, Innocent.

IN the ARTFUL,---the Senſible, Penetrating, Engaging.

IN the INNOCENT,---the Senſible, Modeſt.

I AM conſcious much more may be ſaid upon the ſubject of the beauty of the human face, but I have preſumed only to give a hint of a new practical ſcheme to the public, referring the ultimate deciſion of the principles to the feelings and experience of mankind; and I ſhall reſt extremely pleaſed, if this undertaking ſhall promote a diſcuſſion of the ſubject among the curious. I beg leave to add, that upon the whole I have endeavoured to produce the following effects in all the examples, that is, beauty, expreſſion, and dignity, and all of them in the ſtate of tranquility; for I conceive that the whole ſet may be performed or compoſed in ſuch a manner as to be accompanied with more or leſs of the above properties, and yet ſufficiently varied in the individuals by the proper diſtinction of character.

COLLECTION

COLLECTION

OF THE

Principal Variations of the Human Features.

FOREHEAD.	Nofe.	Mouth.	Chin.	Eye-brow.	Eye.
Variations 4.	12.	16.	2.	12.	16.

FOREHEAD.

Var. 1ft. Straight.
2d. Curved outward.
3d. Curved inward.
4th. Curved inward and outward.

NOSE.

Var. 1ft. Straight, the direction of the noftril at right angles with the ridge of the nofe.
2d. Curved inward, the direction of the noftril at right angles with the ridge of the nofe.
3d. Curved outward, the direction of the noftril at right angles with the ridge of the nofe.
4th. Rifing in the middle, the direction of the noftril at right angles with the ridge of the nofe.
5th. Straight, and in comparifon with Variation 1ft. the noftril afcending a little obliquely from the ridge of the nofe.
6th. Curved inward, and in comparifon with Variation 2d, the noftril afcending a little obliquely from the ridge of the nofe.
7th. Curved outward, and in comparifon with Variation 3d, the noftril afcending a little obliquely from the ridge of the nofe.
8th. Rifing in the middle and in comparifon with Variation 4th, the noftril afcending a little obliquely from the ridge of the nofe.
9th. Straight, and in comparifon with Variation 5th, the noftril afcending a little more obliquely from the ridge of the nofe.
10th. Curved inward, and in comparifon with Variation 6th, the noftril afcending a little more obliquely from the ridge of the nofe.
11th. Curved outward, and in comparifon with Variation 7th, the noftril afcending a little more obliquely from the ridge of the nofe.
12th. Rifing in the middle, and in comparifon with Variation 8th, the noftril afcending a little more obliquely from the ridge of the nofe.

MOUTH.

Var. 1ſt. Upper lip projecting. Thick lips. Upper lip ending toward the middle of the mouth. Under lip ending in the ſame manner.

2d. Upper lip projecting. Thick lips. Upper lip ending toward the middle of the mouth. Under lip ending at the corner of the mouth.

3d. Upper lip projecting. Thick lips. Upper lip ending at the corner of the mouth. Under lip ending toward the middle of the mouth.

4th. Upper lip projecting. Thick lips. Upper lip ending at the corner of the mouth. Under lip ending in the ſame manner.

5th. Upper lip projecting. Thin lips. Upper lip ending toward the middle of the mouth. Under lip ending in the ſame manner.

6th. Upper lip projecting. Thin lips. Upper lip ending toward the middle of the mouth. Under lip ending at the corner.

7th. Upper lip projecting. Thin lips. Upper lip ending at the corner of the mouth. Under lip ending toward the middle of the mouth.

8th. Upper lip projecting. Thin lips. Upper lip ending at the corner of the mouth. Under lip ending in the ſame manner.

9th. Upper lip projecting. Upper lip thin. Under lip thick. Upper lip ending toward the middle of the mouth. Under lip ending in the ſame manner.

10th. Upper lip projecting. Upper lip thin. Under lip thick. Upper lip ending toward the middle of the mouth. Under lip ending at the corner of the mouth.

11th. Upper lip projecting. Upper lip thin. Under lip thick. Upper lip ending at the corner of the mouth. Under lip ending toward the middle of the mouth.

12th. Upper lip projecting. Upper lip thin. Under lip thick. Upper lip ending at the corner of the mouth. Under lip ending in the ſame manner.

13th. Upper lip projecting. Upper lip thick. Under lip thin. Upper lip ending toward the middle of the mouth. Under lip ending in the ſame manner.

14th. Upper lip projecting. Upper lip thick. Under lip thin. Upper lip ending toward the middle of the mouth. Under lip ending at the corner.

15th. Upper lip projecting. Upper lip thick. Under lip thin. Upper lip ending at the corner of the mouth. Under lip ending toward the middle of the mouth.

16th. Upper lip projecting. Upper lip thick. Under lip thin. Upper lip ending at the corner of the mouth. Under lip ending in the ſame manner.

CHIN.

CHIN.

Var. 1ſt. Single.

2d. Double.

EYE-BROW.

Var. 1ſt. Straight, at right angles with the ridge of the noſe.

2d. Straight, deſcending obliquely from the ridge of the noſe.

3d. Straight, aſcending obliquely from the ridge of the noſe.

4th. Curved, at right angles with the ridge of the noſe.

5th. Curved, deſcending obliquely from the ridge of the noſe.

6th. Curved, aſcending obliquely from the ridge of the noſe.

7th. Waving, in poſition, at right angles from the ridge of the noſe. The part next to the noſe curving upward.

8th. Waving, in poſition deſcending from the ridge of the noſe. The part next to the noſe curving upward.

9th. Waving, in poſition aſcending from the ridge of the noſe. The part next to the noſe curving upward.

10th. Waving, in poſition, at right angles with the ridge of the noſe. The part next to the noſe curving downward.

11th. Waving, in poſition deſcending from the ridge of the noſe. The part next to the noſe curving downward.

12th. Waving, in poſition aſcending from the ridge of the noſe. The part next to the noſe curving downward.

EYE.

Var. 1ſt. Cloſe. Upper and under eye-lid broad. Pupil much covered by the upper eye-lid.

2d. Cloſe. Upper and under eye-lid narrow. Pupil much covered by the upper eye-lid.

3d. Cloſe. Upper eye-lid broad. Under eye-lid narrow. Pupil much covered.

4th. Cloſe. Upper eye-lid narrow. Under eye-lid broad. Pupil much covered.

5th. Cloſe. Upper and under eye-lid broad. Pupil a little covered.

6th. Cloſe. Upper and under eye-lid narrow. Pupil a little covered.

7th. Cloſe. Upper eye-lid broad. Under eye-lid narrow. Pupil a little covered.

8th. Cloſe. Upper eye-lid narrow. Under eye-lid broad. Pupil a little covered.

9th. Open. Upper and under eye-lid broad. Pupil much covered.

10th. Open. Upper and under eye-lid narrow. Pupil much covered.

11th. Open. Upper eye-lid broad. Under eye-lid narrow. Pupil much covered.

12th. Open. Upper eye-lid narrow. Under eye-lid broad. Pupil much covered.

13th. Open. Upper and under eye-lid broad. Pupil a little covered.

14th. Open. Upper and under eye-lid narrow. Pupil a little covered.

15th. Open. Upper eye-lid broad. Under eye-lid narrow. Pupil a little covered.

16th. Open. Upper eye-lid narrow. Under eye-lid broad. Pupil a little covered.

TABLES

OF

Various Combinations of the Features.

TABLE I.

Combination of the Features of the SIMPLE BEAUTY.

Forehead, 2d variation. Noſe, 6th. Mouth, 3d. Chin, 1ſt. Eye-brow, 4th. Eye, 12th.

TABLE II.

Of the Features of the MAJESTIC.

Forehead, 1ſt var. Noſe, 5th. Mouth, 4th. Chin, 2d. Eye-brow, 6th. Eye, 13th.

TABLE III.

Of the SENSIBLE, *or* WISE.

Forehead, 1ſt var. Noſe, 3d. Mouth, 4th. Chin, 1ſt. Eye-brow, 6th. Eye, 9th.

TABLE IV.

Of the STEADY.

Forehead, 1ſt var. Noſe, 7th. Mouth, 10th. Chin, 2d. Eye-brow, 10th. Eye, 14th.

TABLE V.

Of the SPIRITED.

Forehead, 4th var. Noſe, 12th. Mouth, 12th. Chin, 1ſt. Eye-brow, 9th. Eye, 14th.

TABLE VI.

Of the HAUGHTY.

Forehead, 1ſt var. Noſe, 12th. Mouth, 4th. Chin, 2d. Eye-brow, 4th. Eye, 9th.

TABLE VII.

Of the MELANCHOLIC.

Forehead, 2d var. Noſe, 9th. Mouth, 10th. Chin, 1ſt. Eye-brow, 8th. Eye, 9th.

TABLE

TABLE VIII.

Of the TENDER.

Forehead, 2d var. Noſe, 6th. Mouth, 12th. Chin, 1ſt. Eye-brow, 11th. Eye, 2d.

TABLE IX.

Of the MODEST.

Forehead, 2d var. Noſe, 5th. Mouth, 12th. Chin, 1ſt. Eye-brow, 4th. Eye, 12th.

TABLE X.

Of the LANGUID, or DELICATE.

Forehead, 2d var. Noſe, 4th. Mouth, 8th. Chin, 1ſt. Eye-brow, 8th. Eye, 12th.

TABLE XI.

Of the PENETRATING.

Forehead, 2d var. Noſe, 6th. Mouth, 6th. Chin, 1ſt. Eye-brow, 1ſt. Eye, 8th.

TABLE XII.

Of the ENGAGING.

Forehead, 2d var. Noſe, 8th. Mouth, 12th. Chin, 2d. Eye-brow, 8th. Eye, 2d.

TABLE XIII.

Of the GOOD-NATURED.

Forehead, 2d var. Noſe, 6th. Mouth, 4th. Chin, 2d. Eye-brow, 5th. Eye, 2d.

TABLE XIV.

Of the TIMID.

Forehead, 2d var. Noſe, 6th. Mouth, 12th. Chin, 1ſt. Eye-brow, 8th. Eye, 14th.

TABLE XV.

Of the CHEARFUL.

Forehead, 2d var. Noſe, 10th. Mouth, 4th. Chin, 2d. Eye-brow, 7th. Eye, 14th.

TABLE XVI.

Of the ARTFUL.

Forehead, 2d var. Noſe, 10th. Mouth, 6th. Chin, 1ſt. Eye-brow, 9th. Eye, 6th.

TABLE XVII.

Of the INNOCENT.

Forehead, 2d var. Noſe, 2d. Mouth, 9th. Chin, 1ſt. Eye-brow, 5th. Eye, 2d.

FINIS.

PRINCIPES

DE

BEAUTÉ,

CONSIDERÉS RÈLATIVEMENT

À LA TÊTE HUMAINE.

Par ALEXANDRE COZENS.

À LONDRES,

Imprimé par JACQUES DIXWELL, No. 148, dans la *Rue St. Martin*, proche *Charing Cross*.

M.DCC.LXXVII.

A U

R O I.

SIRE,

C'EST avec la plus vive reconnoissance pour l'honneur distingué que Votre Majesté a bien voulù me faire en me permettant de Lui dédier l'essai suivant, que j'ose aujourd'hui le mettre a Ses pieds.

Le sentiment que j'éprouve en cette occasion est mêlé de plaisir et de crainte, convaincu, comme je le suis, que je trouverai en Votre Majesté non moins le juge que le protecteur des arts.

Je suis avec le plus profond respect,

SIRE,

De Votre Majesté

Le très obligé, très fidele,

Et très devoué sujet et serviteur,

ALEXANDRE COZENS.

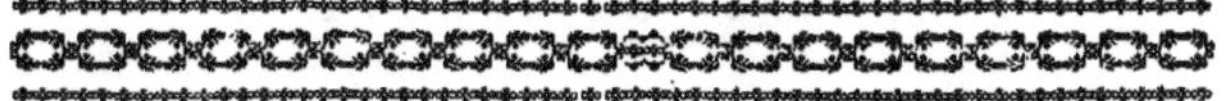

PRINCIPES
DE
BEAUTÉ,
CONSIDERÉS RELATIVEMENT
À LA TÊTE HUMAINE,
&c. &c. &c.

COMME je ne me propose point dans cet ouvrage de traiter philosophiquement de la beauté en général, je n'entrerai dans aucune discussion sur son existance, son origine, sa nature, & ses fins; me contentant de la considérer dans un sens limité; & soumettant mes idées au jugement du public, je tâcherai donc, prémiérement, de démontrer comment on peut former la beauté simple de la face humaine, c'est à dire un beau visage sans caractére; comme aussi la beauté composée, c'est à dire une beauté à laquelle est annexé un caractére; & je me flatte que mon systéme pourra, non seulement plaire aux amateurs, mais encore devenir utile aux praticiens.

Le manque de précision dans les idées qu'on se forme de la beauté a jusqu'ici fait douter s'il existoit telle chose qu'un visage d'une beauté simple & absolue; & il est évident que, tant que cette controverse subsistera, la beauté simple & absolue n'en sçauroit être le sujet. Car, tandis qu'un tel homme préfere un certain assemblage de traits à tout autre, parcequ'il lui donne l'idée de la modestie, qu'un autre admire une contenance qui exprime la bonté d'ame, qu'un troisiéme est transporté à la vûe d'un visage sur lequel est répandû un leger nuage de mélancolie, & ainsi des autres goûts; n'est-il pas clair que tous ces observateurs ont mêlé quelque chose d'étranger et d'hétérogene dans leurs recherches, nommément leurs faintaisies & leurs penchants, et qu'ils ne contestent pas sur la beauté en elle même, mais sur ses modifications dans les divers caractéres de bon, de modeste, et de mélancolique.

B Enfin;

Enfin ; ce n'eſt pas la propoſition qu'ils ont en vûe, mais bien les corollaires qui en reſultent; car tandis qu'ils continuent d'annexer tels et tels caractéres à la beauté, comment peut-elle être ſimple? et tandis qu'ils demeurent dans cette incertitude, et continuent cette diſpute, comment peut-elle être abſolue? Mon ſentiment eſt donc, qu'un certain aſſemblage de traits peut-être combiné par un procédé régulier et déterminé de l'art, lequel produira la beauté ſimple ſans caractére et ſans paſſions. De là, comme d'une harmonieuſe et ſimple piece de muſique, pluſieurs variations peuvent être derivées, par certain arrangement de traits exprimant les divers caractéres, ou mouvemens de l'ame ; ce qui, à la vérité s'éloignera du principe de ſimple beauté, mais ne s'y trouvera point incompatible.

Je me propoſe de mettre ce ſyſtéme dans tout ſon jour par la méthode ſuivante.

Prémiérement, en donnant une collection des traits humains, pris séparément, et déſſinés en contours de profil, et de grandeur naturelle.

Secondement, par des tables des diverſes combinaiſons de ces traits choiſis dans la collection ſuſdite, et tout prêts à être employés pour la compoſition des viſages. La prémiére table conſiſtant dans ces traits qui expriment la beauté ſimple, et les autres tables conſiſtant en ces traits qui expriment les beautès caractérisées ; comme la majeſtueuſe, la ſpirituelle, &c. *

Troiſiémement, en donnant l'exemple d'un viſage de profil tiré en contours, et ſelon la prémiére table, dans laquelle j'ai choiſi les traits qui expriment la beauté ſimple ;

Et d'autres exemples de viſages deſſinès de la même manière, et d'aprés des tables dans leſquelles j'ai choiſi les traits qui expriment les beautès caractériſées.

A chacun de ces viſages, j'ai adapté une cœffure, tracée dans le ſtyle de l'antique, et imprimée ſur une feuille d'un papier ſi mince qu'on peut voir à travers le viſage auquel elle ſied.

En formant ces modéles, et en ſuivant les gradations délicates des caractéres qui conviennent à la beauté dénuée de paſſions, j'ai employé toute l'attention et toute l'habileté dont je ſuis capable ; cependant, comme des touches plus parſaites, une plus juſte expreſſion, peuvent avoir été produites par des talens ſupérieurs aux miens, je m'en remets à l'indulgence du public. Qu'il me ſoit, néanmoins permis d'obſerver que, comme c'eſt le vrai plutôt que l'élégance, le précepte plutôt que la pratique que je deſire ſaire entendre par mon ſyſtéme, il y a lieu d'eſpérer que, pourvû que je ne manque pas de clarté, on excuſera ſans peine quelques fautes d'exécution. Sur cette conſidération, et craignant que la nouveauté et la nature de mes principes ne jettaſſent de l'obſcurité dans mes phraſes, j'ai cherché à parler aux yeux par des exemples, comptant d'obvier à tout par ce moyen lequel eſt, en effet, le plus propre, non ſeulement pour expliquer, mais encore pour démontrer les principes les plus abſtraits.

* Qu'il me ſoit ici permis d'offrir une idée : ne pourroit-on pas de la même manière faire des tables de traits tirés des têtes antiques ? je dis plus, ne pourroit-on pas aller juſqu'à copier la nature dans la compoſition des viſages d'après de viſages réels. J'ai moi même fait une table des traits de la Vénus de Medicis ; et d'autres que moi peuvent s'amuſer à de pareils eſſais.

Il me reste donc à faire voir par des exemples qu'il peut y avoir un certain assemblage ou combinaison de traits, qui constitue, ou compose, la beauté simple, définie comme cy dessus, sans caractére prédominant, sans affection particuliére, et totalement dénuée de passion.

Que de cette simple forme procédent plusieurs branches de beauté composée, c'est à dire, la beauté simple avec une addition d'affections et de caractéres; et ceci, je m'efforcerai de le prouver par des exemples.

Il faut avoüer que, quand ces beautés composées, ou charactérisées, frappent les observateurs, diverses opinions, et différens goûts s'en ensuivent, vû la préférence que chacun d'eux donne à un caractére, ou style de beauté, plutôt qu'à un autre; mais cette varieté d'opinions n'a aucun rapport avec la beauté simplement considerée; elle roule sur les différens modes dont cette beauté est susceptible, lesquels sont moins apperçûs par les yeux que senti par le cœur.

Il est sous entendû que cette addition de caractéres doit être marquée si délicatement qu'on n'y voïe aucun degré de passion, et que la beauté, qui doit toujours prédominer, n'en soit pas affoiblie. Je procedérai donc dans la liste des exemples dans une sorte de gradation, depuis le genre le plus dignifié, ou supérieur, jusqu'au plus familier, ou inférieur, et en me bornant à la beauté des femmes; quoique les principes sur lesquels ces essais sont fondès soïent applicables à la tête humaine, en général, et pour les deux sexes.

En considérant avec attention les différentes espéces et le nombre de caractéres humains qui peuvent s'accorder avec la beauté, il m'a parû qu'on peut les comprendre sous les dénominations suivantes, seize en nombre.

La Majestueuse.	La Languissante, ou Délicate.
La Spirituelle, ou Sensée, ou Judicieuse.	L'Intelligente, ou Pénétrante.
La Décidée, ou Ferme, ou Déterminée.	La Prévenante, ou Engageante.
La Vive.	La Douce, ou Sociable.
La Fiére, ou Hautaine.	La Craintive.
La Mélancolique.	La Gaïe.
La Sensible, ou Tendre.	La Fine, ou Rusée, ou Adroite.
La Timide.	L'Innocente.

Ce sont là toutes les classes de beautés qui me paroissent entrer dans la définition et limitation de la beaute caracterisée et indépendante de passion; car, je dois le répéter, ce n'est point les passions que j'ai actuellement en vûe.

Je crois ici devoir expliquer ou définir l'idée que j'attache aux epithetes qui je viens de donner aux beautés caractérisées. Traiter cette matiére à fond seroit une tâche trop longue pour mon dessein actuel; ainsi je dirai ce que j'en pense de la manière la plus concise qu'il me sera possible. J'observerai, cependant, que par chacune de ces qualitès humaines que les desdites épithetes désignent, j'entens une habitude fixe de l'ame et non une situation momentanée de l'esprit.

Par la Majestueuse, j'entens une dignité procédant d'une conviction intime d'independance.

Par la Spirituelle, ou Sensée, j'entens une capacité, ou force de raison.

Par la Decidée, ou Ferme, j'entens une qualité fondée sur la résolution d'être ferme, en distinction de la tranquillité machinale.

Par la Vive, j'entens le résultat d'un mouvement constant et rapide des esprits animaux.

Par la Fiére, ou Hautaine, j'entens une dignité qu'on s'arroge, en contradiction de la Majestueuse.

Par la Mélancolique, j'entens un abbatement d'esprit, provenant de chagrins répétés.

Par la Sensible, ou Tendre, j'entens une ame qui sent vivement; et s'emeut facilement.

Par la Timide, j'entens un esprit qui se défie de lui même.

Par la Languissante, ou Délicate, j'entens une délicatesse de temperemment.

Par la Pénétrante, ou Intelligente, j'entens une perspicuité et vitesse dans les perceptions.

Par la Prévenante, ou Engageante, j'entens le desir de plaire.

Par la Douce, ou Sociable, j'entens une douceur de caractére.

Par la Craintive, j'entens une habitude produite par l'apprehension fréquente de mauvais traitements.

Par la Gaïe, j'entens une personne de belle humeur et encline à la joie.

Par la Fine, ou la Rusée, ou Adroite, j'entens une manière perçante d'examiner les choses avec l'intention d'en faire son profit.

Par l'Innocente, j'entens un caractére inoffensif, et incapable de soupçonner le mal.

On peut observer dans la face humaine, en général, que la nature a assigné un lieu particulier pour chacun des effets suivants, viz. beauté, expression, dignité. De là j'avancerai, que

que, c'eſt le front et le nez qui conſtituent la beauté, que l'expreſſion s'annonce par les yeux et la bouche, et que la dignité ſiège ſur le menton, et quelquefois ſur le front et le nez, conjointement; ce qu'on pourroit aisément prouver par des exemples tirés des têtes antiques.

On peut ici hazarder une conjecture; c'eſt, que ce qui eſt appellé le nez droit des Grecs, lequel eſt regardé comme le modele du beau à cet égard, procéde d'un manque d'attention dans l'examen. L'idée de l'auteur ſur ce point eſt celle ci; que dans les lignes légerement courbées de la beauté, telles qu'elles ſe trouvent dans le front, le nez, &c. celles qui s'éloignent le moins de la ligne droite ſont les plus belles. Les anciens ont executé ces eſpéces de lignes, que j'appelle inſenſiblement courbées, en formant le trait en queſtion (le nez) en telle maniére que leur déviation de la ligne droite etant preſque imperceptible, elles paroiſſent être toutes entierement droites à la pluſpart des obſervateurs qui ne ſaiſiſſent pas ces délicates variations; et de là eſt probablement venûe la commune opinion que, le nez Grec etant droit, il eſt le modele du goût pour ce trait.

De ce qui a été dit en général, je penſe qu'on peut établir comme un principe, "Que, "la beauté et le caractére du viſage conſiſtent en la forme et la couleur; mais que la paſſion "et les graces dépendent de l'action." La derniere partie de cette propoſition eſt ainſi entendue par Milton, quand il dit,

> On voïoit de la grace dans tous ſes mouvemens, le ciel dans ſes yeux,
> De la dignité et de l'amour dans ſes moindres geſtes.

Et Homère dans ſes deſcriptions d'Appollon ne manque pas de le peindre en action, comme le moïen le plus propre à exprimer ſa grace divine; tandis que plus conformement au caractére de Jupiter, il le repreſente recueilli et tranquille.

Quoique la varieté qui ſe trouve dans les beaux viſages ſoit évidente, cependant nous ne pouvons pas immédiatement deviner la diſtinction particuliére qui eſt entre eux de manière à pouvoir y donner un nom. Ceci eſt causé par la délicate liaiſon des caractéres avec la beauté, qui leur communique à tous un certain degré de reſſemblance; et rend ces diſtinctions preſque imperceptibles dans leur nuances légéres. Si cet effet eſt apperçu dans tous les exemples de cet ouvrage, on conviendra, j'eſpére, que j'aurai copié la nature à cet égard.

Des milliers de combinaiſons de traits peuvent ſe faire, parmi leſquelles il y en aura pluſieurs vuide de caractére, comme auſſi de beauté, mais donnant certaines ideés de contenances mixtes (comme on en voit tous les jours dans le cours de la vie,) cependant d'autres pourront exprimer tout enſemble la beauté et les caractéres, et probablement un plus grand degré de vérité qu'il ne s'en trouve dans les exemples ci joint. Cette expérience eſt abandonée au public en général. Dans la vûe de faciliter cet eſſai, l'ouvrage préſent eſt arrangé de manière que, qui-conque voudra l'étudier pourra s'amuſer à former de nouvelles idées de faces humaines en combinant les traits en différentes ſortes.

La méthode dont je fis d'abord usage fut d'établir et de déterminer l'idée de la beauté simple, en choisissant les traits de la collection qui je crois doit produire cette idèe. Après quoi je traçai ces traits choisis l'un après l'autre dans leurs propres places, commençant par le front, à travers d'une feuille de papier mince & transparent. Les contours de la beauté simple etant ainsi achevès, j'en fis usage comme d'un plan ou canevas pour former les subséquentes beautés caractérisées. En exécutant chacun de ces modéles je plaçai, une feuille de papier très mince sur ces contours de la beauté simple, & en changeai les traits pour ceux de la collection qui me paroissoit tendre à exprimer le caractère ou espéce de beauté que j'avois en vûe. M'étant aussi convaincû que l'expression des visages, peut-être considérablement augmentée par la cœffure, je composai autant de cœffures qu'il y a de visages, les plaçant ou je presumai qu'elles seroient le mieux adaptées, dans l'intention qu'elles fussent appliquées aux visages, & arrangées de manière à produire l'effet le plus convenable. Je les ai donc faites imprimer sur un papier transparent, & n'ai pas voulû les faire relier avec le reste du livre, afin de donner le moïen de les mouvoir à plaisir sur quelque face que ce soit, et de les appliquer à toutes les faces, selon qu'on le trouveroit bon.

Qu'on me permette d'observer que j'ai tout exprès rejetté toute assistance collatérale qui eût pû prévenir des yeux ordinaires en faveur de ces desseins & de ces exemples; comme les ombres, les traits adoucis & libres, &c. Ceci reconnû, le mérite de ces exemples restera établi sur le fondement des contours seulement, contours que j'ai même jugé à propos de tracer d'une manière qui approche de la précision mathematicale. C'étoit là mettre mon systéme à la plus sévére des épreuves, & c'est ce que je desire; mais je souhaiterois ardemment que quelque sculpteur habile trouva qu'il vaudroit la peine de donner un assortiment parfait d'exemples de la beauté simple & des beautès caractérisées, en modèle de terre glaize (ou de plâtre), ou executés en marbre, afin qu'ils servissent comme de modèles pour la beautès dans les siécles futurs.

En approfondissant ce sujet, j'ai été entrainé aux observations suivantes, que j'ose offrir au public.

La beauté simple de la face humaine est unique, & la même dans tous les tems & dans tous les lieux, & elle est denuée de tout caractére intellectuel & prédominant. Ceci procéde de certaines proprietès dans l'objet, qui sont expressement convenables à faire naître cette idée, l'examen desquelles je n'entreprens point. Ainsi, si toutes les femmes avoient une beauté simple elles se ressembleroient toutes entre elles. Cette extreme simplicité de contenance étoit probablement très marquée dans Eve, dont l'ame, non préoccupée, est décrite par Milton dans les lignes suivantes de son Paradis perdû, lesqu'elles sont données ici avec très peu d'altérations.

Ce jour (je me le rappelle souvent) que sortant d'un profond sommeil
Je m'eveillai pour la prémiére fois, et me trouvai couchée
A l'ombre sur des fleurs, ne sachant point où j'étois,
Et qui j'étois, d'où, et pourquoi l'on m'avoit portée en ce lieu.

Quant

Quant aux caractéres de la beauté simple, ils sont frappants dans la description qu'Adam fait d'Eve au moment de sa création, lorsqu'il dit dans le même poéme ;

" Sous sa main créatice un être se format ;
" Il étoit semblable à l'homme, mais différoit en sexe,
" Mais se trouvoit si aimable et si beau,
" Que tout ce qu'il y avoit de beau dans le monde sembloit
" Vil alors, ou plutôt étoit rassemblé, et combiné en elle
" Et dans ses regards.

La beauté simple peut être comparée à une eau pure et élementaire, & le caractére est à la beauté ce que sont la saveur, l'odeur, & la couleur à l'eau, qui par l'addition de diverses infusions, seroit appellée douce, ou aigre, parfumée, ou jaune ou rouge, &c. toutes différentes espéces ou sortes d'eau ; car l'addition de caractére donne à la beauté une qualité distinctive, produisant tous les différent genres de beautés caractérisées, chacune également agréable quant à l'effet qu'elles ont sur les différents goûts du genre humain, mais inférieure à la beauté simple par rapport à sa pureté, ainsi, comme je suppose qu'il existe une eau élémentaire, je présume aussi qu'il y a une beauté élémentaire, laquelle ne dépend ni du goût, ni de la prévention, mais qui peut recevoir l'alliage d'autres qualités. Comme l'eau peut-être mêlée avec le vin ou le lait, &c. dans le même verre ; de même la beauté avec l'expression de la majesté, ou avec celle du bon sens, peut-être combinée dans le même visage. L'infusion donne la saveur ou l'expression à l'insipide élément ; & on peut observer que quelques caractéres s'unissent plus intimément à la beauté que d'autres, tandis qu'on conçoit aisémement que la fermeté & la ruse s'accordent moins avec la beauté que ne le sont la modestie et la douceur, &c. De là il paroitroit que la beauté simple est pure, parcequ'elle n'a point de caractére, et que les beautés caractérisées sont en quelque dégré (si l'on peut ainsi s'exprimer) impures, parce que leur beauté n'est pas simple et sans mélange.

En consequence de ces observations, la beauté est, dans un sens, invariable, comme dans la beauté simple, et, dans un autre sens, elle est variée, comme dans les beautés caractérisées (prenant toute la suite ensemble) et de plus il est probable qu'il est ordonné que parmi les hommes il se trouveroit certaines especes de goûts et de fantaisies adaptées aux diverses espéces de beautés caractérisées ; (sur ce fondement on peut établir toutes les différentes opinions locales sur la beauté, comme la Chinoise, l'Ethiopienne, l'Hottentote, &c. quoique l'extravagance de quelques uns de ces goûts nous paroisse, à nous Européens, s'éloigner de la beauté simple jusqu'à la difformité ;) et de même, qu'il y a des hommes qui possedent une force de discernement qui les rend capables d'appercevoir la beauté simple et sans mélange. En d'autres mots, qu'il y a des classes d'hommes qui etant respectivement attachés à chacune des beautés caractérisées, ne seront point frappès à l'aspect de la beauté simple, et qu'il y a une autre classe d'hommes que leur discernement et leur goût delicat portent à admirer la beauté simple, et cette classe trouvera les beautés caractérisées imparfaites. J'ai du penchant à croire que la beauté simple échape, par son insipidité, à l'attention des hommes, qui, vû leurs occupations, passions, habitudes, ou coutumes, sont mal disposés pour la discerner, et sur lesquels, quand ils la discernent, elle ne fait, à cause des susdites préventions, qu'une impression passagére; semblables à ceux qui s'étant accoutumès à boire des liqueurs fortes ne peuvent plus savourer la pureté de l'eau. On peut donc présumer que les personnes qui sont les plus capables d'appercevoir la beauté simple sont celles qui sont le plus libres de l'embarras des affaires, de l'influence des passions, d'habitudes invétérées, et de vieilles coutumes.

L'effet que la beauté simple produit sur le spectateur est l'admiration, mélée avec le plaisir dans l'amusement que sa vûe lui fournit; les beautés caracterisées font naître d'autres sortes d'émotions qui tendent à interesser les passions. Ici j'ai casuellement remarqué que la beauté simple de la face humaine posséde la singuliére proprieté d'amuser l'observateur curieux en lui faisant croire ou imaginer qu'un certain visage a en soi, ou peut prendre, avec l'addition de l'habitude, le caractére qui s'allie avec son propre goût; pensée qui l'engage à s'approuver lui même comme aiant fait une découverte. Un autre observateur curieux peut s'amuser de la même manière en regardent le même visage, & s'imaginant d'y trouver une capacité qui tend à un caractére entiérement de son goût, mais totalement différent de celui qu'un autre y a apperçu. Ainsi la beauté simple peut fournir un fond de ce genre à des spectateurs de presque tous les goûts.

La beauté simple, telle que je la suppose exister dans la nature, ne peut servir de modéle pour aucun ouvrage de l'art, parce qu'il est peut-être impossible aux facultés humaines de la trouver pure. L'exemple donné ici de la beauté simple est seulement mis à la place de cette beauté qu'il est si difficile de trouver dans la nature. Cependant, de frequents essais pour parvenir à cette découverte, faits par des personnes parfaitement intelligentes, peuvent produire quelques echantillons, ou exemples, qui se rapprocheront de plus en plus du point de la beauté pure et simple.

A l'égard de l'objection, que l'application de cet ouvrage à la pratique, ne resserre ou ne reprime le génie; on peut répondre, que nonobstant les principes méchaniques sur lesquels ce systéme est établi, il ne s'ensuivra pas qu'un peintre, ou statuaire, puisse, seulement en y adhérant, produire une representation de la beauté ou du caractére, mais il peut du moins en être assisté. En effet, ces représentations dépendent non seulement des belles formes ou des différentes variations des traits, mais encore de leur assortiment, position, proportions et comparaisons; et qui ne voit que l'ajustement de tout cela est du ressort du génie. Cette circonstance offre donc la plus grande étendue au goût et au jugement du dessinateur, tandis qu'il n'est pas au pouvoir des principes de mettre des bornes au génie.

La

La beauté miſe en comparaiſon avec la difformité admet une gradation; c'eſt à dire, une petite déviation de la beauté ſimple eſt un degré de difformité, comme une petite déviation de la lumiére eſt un degré de tenebres. Mais entre la beauté ſimple& la difformité un certain point eſt ſupposé, & toutes les déviations de la beauté ſimple vers ce point ſont regardées comme des différents degrés de beauté, tandis que tous les degrés de ce point vers l'extreme difformité, ſont appellès degrés de difformité; mais il y a un plus grand nombre de degrés de difformité que de ceux de beauté, parcequ'il ſe trouve beaucoup plus de formes qu'il ne s'en trouve de régulieres. Pour cette raiſon il ſeroit, peut-être, plus difficile de trouver un modèle pour l'extreme difformité qu'il ne l'eſt pour la beauté ſimple.

Dans la cours de mes obſervations ſur les divers genres de beaux viſages, et dans mes fréquents examens des exemples que j'en donne dans cet ouvrage, un effet, ou apparence, dans la contenance humaine s'eſt preſenté à mes yeux, lequel eſt peut-être nouveau, et peut devenir utile pour l'art de deſſiner. J'offrirai donc cette obſervation accidentelle au public dans le même jour dont j'ai été frappé, & je ſoumettrai la vérité et l'exatitude de la propoſition au jugement reflechi des curieux qui décideront, du moins, s'il y a quelque choſe de réel dans ma conjecture. Voici dequoi il eſt queſtion. En prémier lieu, le viſage de la beauté ſimple ſemble expoſer aux yeux quelque foible apparence de tous les caractéres que j'ai décrits comme appartenant à l'ame, excepté trois, la vive, la fiere, & la fine, tout ainſi que la lumière, ſelon Newton, contient toutes les couleurs priſmatiques. Secondement, dans tous les viſages des beautés caractériſées on peut remarquer un petit degré de reſſemblance entre elles. J'eſpére que l'obſcurité qui eſt ici inévitable ſera éclaircie par l'arrangement ſuivant.

Dans la Beauté Simple on peut voir quelque petit degré de-là Majeſteuſe; de la Spirituelle, ou Senſée, ou Judicieuſe; de la Décidée, ou Déterminée, ou Ferme; de la Mélancolique; de la Senſible, ou Tendre; de la Timide; de la Languiſſante, ou Délicate; de la Pénétrante, ou Intelligente; de la Prévenante, ou Engageante; de la Douce, ou Sociable; de la Craintive; de la Gaïe; de l'Innocente.

Dans la Majeſtueuſe on peut voir en un petite degré de la Spirituelle, ou Senſée, ou Judicieuſe; de la Ferme, ou Déterminée, ou Décidée; de la Vive; de la Fiére, ou Hautaine; de la Pénétrante, ou Intelligente; de la Douce ou Sociable.

Dans la Spirituelle, ou Sensée, ou Judicieuſe, eſt la Majeſtueuſe; la Déterminée, ou Ferme, ou Décidée; la Pénétrante, ou Intelligente.

Dans la Déterminée, ou Ferme, eſt la Majeſtueuſe; la Spirituelle, ou Sensée, ou Judicieuſe; la Fière; la Pénétrante, ou Intelligente.

Dans la Vive, eſt la Majeſtueuſe; la Spirituelle, ou Sensée, ou Judicieuſe; la Ferme, ou Déterminée, ou Décidée; l'Intelligente ou Pénétrante.

Dans la Fière, ou Hautaine, est la Majestueuse; la Spirituelle, ou Sensée, ou Judicieuse; la Décidée, ou Ferme, ou Déterminée.

Dans la Mélancolique, est la Spirituelle, ou Judicieuse, ou Sensée; la Timide; la Languissante, ou Délicate.

Dans la Sensible, ou Tendre, est la Spirituelle, ou Sensée, ou Judicieuse; la Mélancolique; la Timide; la Languissante, ou Delicate; l'Intelligente, ou Pénétrante; la Douce, ou Sociable; la Craintive; l'Innocente.

Dans la Timide, est la Spirituelle, ou Sensée, ou Judicieuse; la Douce, ou Sociable; la Craintive, l'Innocente.

Dans la Languissante, ou Délicate, est la Spirituelle, ou Sensée, ou Judicieuse; la Timide; la Craintive.

Dans l'Intelligente, ou Pénétrante, est la Spirituelle, ou Sensée, ou Judicieuse; la Vive.

Dans la Prévénante, ou Engageante, est la Spirituelle, ou Sensée, ou Judicieuse; la Vive; la Pénétrante, ou Intelligente; la Douce, ou Sociable; la Rusée, ou Fine, ou Adroite.

Dans la Douce, ou Sociable, est la Spirituelle, ou Sensée, ou Judicieuse; la Gaïe; l'Innocente.

Dans la Craintive, est la Spirituelle, ou Sensée, ou Judicieuse; la Sensible, ou Tendre; la Timide; la Pénétrante, ou Intelligente.

Dans la Gaïe, est la Spirituelle, ou Sensée, ou Judicieuse; la Douce, ou Sociable; l'Innocente.

Dans la Fine, ou Adroite, ou Rusée, est, la Spirituelle, ou Sensée, ou Judicieuse; l'Intelligente ou Pénétrante; la Prévenante, ou Engageante.

Dans l'Innocente, est, la Spirituelle, ou Sensée, ou Judicieuse; la Timide.

Je sais qu'on pourroit en dire beaucoup plus que je n'en dis sur la beauté de la face humaine; mais je n'ai prétendû donner simplement que l'idée d'un projet pratique nouveau; référant l'entière décision des principes au sentiment et à l'experience; & je serai très satisfait si mon entreprise excite les curieux à discuter ce sujet. Qu'on me permette d'ajouter que surtout j'ai tâché de produire les effets suivans dans tous les exemples, c'est à dire, la beauté, l'expression, et la dignité; & chacun de ces effets dans l'état de tranquillité; car je conçois que l'entier assortiment peut-être executé ou composé en telle maniére qu'il seroit accompagné de plus ou moins des susdites proprietès, lesquelles seroient pourtant suffisamment variées dans les individus par la distinction de caractéres.

COLLECTION

COLLECTION

DES

Principales Variations des Traits Humains.

LE Front.	Le Nez.	La Bouche.	Le Menton.	Le Sourcil.	L'œil.
Variations 4.	12.	16.	2.	12.	16.

Le FRONT.

Var. 1ſt. Droit.
2. Courbé en dehors.
3. Courbé en dedans.
4. Courbé en dedans & en dehors.

Le NEZ.

Var. 1. Droit, la direction de-la narine à angles droits avec le fil, ou partie ſupérieure du nez.
2. Courbé en dedans, la direction de la narine à angles droits avec le fil du nez.
3. Courbé en dehors, la direction de la narine à angles droits avec le fil du nez.
4. S'élevant dans le milieu, la direction de la narine à angles droits avec le fil du nez.
5. Droit, & en comparaiſon de la variation 1. montant un peu obliquement du fil du nez.
6. Courbé en dedans, & en comparaiſon de la variation 2. la narine montant un peu obliquement du fil du nez.
7. Courbé en dehors, & en comparaiſon de la variation 3. la narine montant un peu obliquement du fil du nez.
8. S'élevant dans la milieu, & en comparaiſon de la 4. variation montant un peu obliquement du fil du nez.
9. Droit, & en comparaiſon de la variation 5. la narine montant un peu plus obliquement du fil du nez.
10. Courbé en dedans, & en comparaiſon de la variation 6. la narine montant un peu obliquement du fil du nez.
11. Courbé en dehors, & en comparaiſon de la variation 7. la narine montant un peu plus obliquement du fil du nez.
12. S'élevant dans le milieu, & en comparaiſon de la variation 8. la narine montant un peu plus obliquement du fil du nez.

La BOUCHE.

Var. 1. La lévre ſupérieure s'avançant, lévres épaiſſes, la lévre ſupérieure finiſſant vers le milieu de la bouche, la lévre inférieure finiſſant en la même manière.

2. La lévre ſupérieure s'avançant, lévres épaiſſes, la lévre ſupérieure finiſſant vers le milieu de la bouche, la lévre inférieure ſiniſſant vers le coin de la bouche.

3. La lévre ſupérieure s'avançant, lévres épaiſſes, la lévre ſupérieure finiſſant vers le coin de la bouche, la lévre inférieure finiſſant vers le milieu de la bouche.

4. La lévre ſupérieure s'avançant, lévres épaiſſes, la lévre ſupérieure finiſſant au coin de la bouche, la lévre inférieure finiſſant en le même manière.

5. La lévre ſupérieure s'avançant, lévres minces, la lévre de deſſus finiſſant vers le milieu de la bouche, la lévre inférieure finiſſant en la même manière.

6. La lévre ſupérieure s'avançant, lévres minces, la lévre ſupérieure finiſſant vers la milieu de la bouche, la lévre inférieure finiſſant au coin de la bouche.

7. La lévre ſupérieure s'avançant, lévres minces, la lévre ſupérieure finiſſant au coin de la bouche, la lévre inférieure finiſſant vers le milieu de la bouche.

8. La lévre ſupérieure s'avançant, lévres minces, le lévre ſupérieure finiſſant au coin de la bouche, le lévre inférieure finiſſant en la même manière.

9. La lévre ſupérieure s'avançant, la lévre ſupérieure mince, la lévre inférieure épaiſſe, la lévre ſupérieure finiſſant vers le milieu de la bouche, la lévre inférieure finiſſant en la même manière.

10. La lévre ſupérieure s'avançant, la lévre ſupérieure mince, la lévre inférieure épaiſſe, la lévre ſupérieure finiſſant vers le milieu de la bouche, la lévre inférieure finiſſant au coin de la bouche.

11. La lévre ſupérieure s'avançant, la lévre ſupérieure mince, la lévre inférieure épaiſſe, la lévre ſupérieure finiſſant au coin de la bouche, la lévre inférieure finiſſant vers le milieu de la bouche.

12. La lévre ſupérieure s'avançant, le lévre ſupérieure mince, la lévre inférieure épaiſſe, la lévre ſupérieure finiſſant au coin de la bouche, la lévre inférieure finiſſant en la même manière.

13. La lévre ſupérieure s'avançant, la lévre ſupérieure épaiſſe, la lévre inférieure mince, la lévre ſupérieure finiſſant vers le milieu de la bouche, la lévre inférieure finiſſant en la même manière.

14. La lévre ſupérieure s'avançant, la lévre ſupérieure épaiſſe, la lévre inférieure mince, la lévre ſupérieure finiſſant vers le milieu de la bouche, le lévre inférieure finiſſant au coin de la bouche.

15. La lévre ſupérieure s'avançant, la lévre ſupérieure épaiſſe, la lévre inférieure mince, la lévre ſupérieure finiſſant au coin de la bouche, la lévre inférieure finiſſant vers le milieu de la bouche.

16. La lévre ſupérieure s'avançant, la lévre ſupérieure épaiſſe, la lévre inférieure mince, la lévre ſupérieure finiſſant au coin de la bouche, la lévre inférieure finiſſant en la même manière.

Le MENTON.

Var. 1. Simple, ou un feul menton.

2. Double, ou un double menton.

Le SOURCIL.

Var. 1. Droit, à angles droits avec le fil, ou partie fupérieure du nez.

2. Droit, defcendant obliquement du fil du nez.

3. Droit, montant obliquement du fil du nez.

4. Courbé à angles droits avec le fil du nez.

5. Courbé, defcendant obliquement du fil du nez.

6. Courbé, montant obliquement du fil du nez.

7. Ondoyant, en pofition, à angles droits avec le fil du nez; la partie prochaine du nez courbée en haut.

8. Ondoyant, en pofition defcendant du fil du nez depuis le commencement; la partie prochaine du nez courbée en haut.

9. Une ondoyante ligne, en pofition montant du fil du nez; la partie prochaine du nez recourbée en haut.

10. Une ligne ondoyante, en pofition, à angles droits avec le fil du nez; la partie prochaine du nez courbée en bas.

11. Une ligne ondoyante, en pofition defcendant du fil du nez; la partie prochaine du nez courbée en bas.

12. Une ligne ondoyante, en pofition montant du fil du nez; la partie prochaine du nez courbée en bas.

L'OE I L.

Var. 1. A demi fermé, la paupiére de deffus et celle de deffous larges, la prunelle très couverte par la paupiére de deffus.

2. A demi fermé, les deux paupiéres étroites, la prunelle très couverte par la paupiére de deffus.

3. A demi fermé, la paupiere de deffus large, la paupiére de deffous étroite, la prunelle très couverte.

4. A demi fermé, la paupiére de deffus étroite, la paupiére de deffous large, la prunelle très couverte.

5. A demi fermé, les deux paupiéres larges, la prunelle un peu couverte.

6. A demi fermé, les deux paupiéres étroites, la prunelle un peu couverte.

7. A demi fermé, la paupiére de deffus large, la paupiére de deffous étroite, la prunelle un peu couverte.

8. A demi fermé, la paupiére de deffus étroite, la paupiére de deffous large, la prunelle un peu couverte.

9. Ouvert, les deux paupiéres larges, la prunelle très couverte.

10. Ouvert, les deux paupiéres étroites, la prunelle très couverte.

11. Ouvert, la paupiére de deffus large, la paupiére de deffous étroite, la prunelle très couverte.

12. Ouvert, la paupiére de deffus étroite, la paupiére de deffous large, la prunelle très couverte.

13. Ouvert, les deux paupiéres larges, la prunelle un peu couverte.

14. Ouvert, les deux paupiéres étroites, la prunelle un peu couverte.

15. Ouvert, la paupiére de deffus large, la paupiére de deffous étroite, la prunelle un peu couverte.

16. Ouvert, la paupiére de deffus étroite, la paupiére de deffous large, la prunelle un peu couverte.

TABLES

DES

Diverſes Combinaiſons de TRAITS.

TABLE I.

Les Traits de la Beauté Simple.

Le Front, 2. var. le Nez, 6. la Bouche, 3. le Menton, 1. le Sourcil, 4. l'œil, 12.

TABLE II.

Les Traits de la Majeſtueuſe.

Le Front, 1. var. le Nez, 5. la Bouche, 4. le Menton, 2. le Sourcil, 6. l'œil, 3.

TABLE III.

La Spirituelle, ou Sensée, ou Judicieuſe.

Le Front, 1. var. le Nez, 3. la Bouche, 4. le Menton, 1. le Sourcil, 6. l'œil, 9.

TABLE IV.

La Déterminée, ou Ferme, ou Décidée.

Le Front, 1. var. le Nez, 7. la Bouche, 10. le Menton, 2. le Sourcil, 10. l'œil, 14.

TABLE V.

De la Vive.

Le Front, 4. var. le Nez, 12. la Bouche, 12. le Menton, 1. le Sourcil, 9. l'œil, 14.

TABLE VI.

De la Fiére, ou Hautaine.

Le Front, 1. var. le Nez, 12. la Bouche, 4. le Menton, 2. le Sourcil, 4. l'œil, 9.

TABLE VII.

De la Mélancolique.

Le Front, 2. var. le Nez, 5. la Bouche, 10. le Menton, 1. le Sourcil, 8 l'œil, 9.

TABLE

TABLE VIII.

De la Sensible, ou Tendre.

Le Front, 2. var. le Nez, 6. la Bouche, 12. le Menton, 1. le Sourcil, 11. l'œil, 2.

TABLE IX.

De la Timide.

Le Front, 2. var. le Nez, 5. la Bouche, 12. le Menton, 1. le Sourcil, 4. l'œil, 12.

TABLE X.

De la Languissante, ou Délicate.

Le Front, 2. var. le Nez, 4. la Bouche, 8. le Menton, 1. le Sourcil, 8. l'œil, 12.

TABLE XI.

De la Pénétrante, ou Intelligente.

Le Front, 2. var. le Nez, 6. la Bouche, 6. le Menton, 1. le Sourcil, 1. l'œil, 8.

TABLE XII.

De la Prévenante, ou Engageante.

Le Front, 2. var. le Nez, 8. la Bouche, 12. le Menton, 2. le Sourcil, 8. l'œil, 2.

TABLE XIII.

De la Douce, ou Sociable.

Le Front, 2. var. le Nez, 6. la Bouche, 4. le Menton, 2. le Sourcil, 5. l'œil, 2.

TABLE XIV.

De la Craintive.

Le Front, 2. var. le Nez, 6. la Bouche, 12. le Menton, 1. le Sourcil, 8. l'œil, 14.

TABLE XV.

De la Gaïe.

Le Front, 2. var. le Nez, 10. la Bouche, 4. le Menton, 2. le Sourcil, 7. l'œil, 14.

TABLE XVI.

De la Fine, ou Rusée, ou Adroite.

Le Front, 2. var. le Nez, 10. la Bouche, 6. le Menton, 1. le Sourcil, 7. l'œil, 6.

TABLE XVII.

De l'Innocente.

Le Front, 2. var. le Nez, 2. la Bouche, 9. la Menton, 1. la Sourcil, 5. l'œil, 2.

FIN.

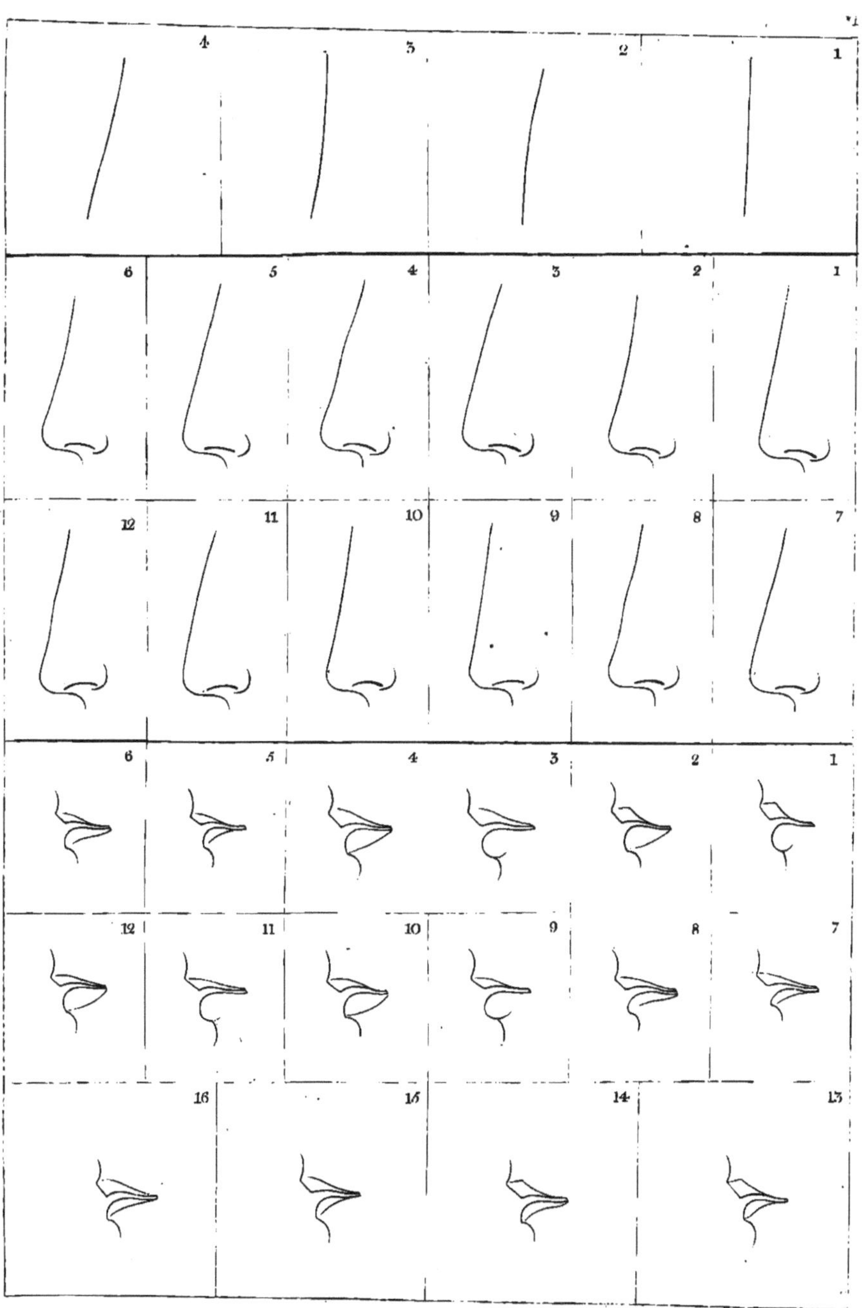

A. Cozens inv. Publish'd April 10. 1777. by Alex.r Cozens, Leicester Street, Leicester Fields, London F. Bartolozzi sculp.

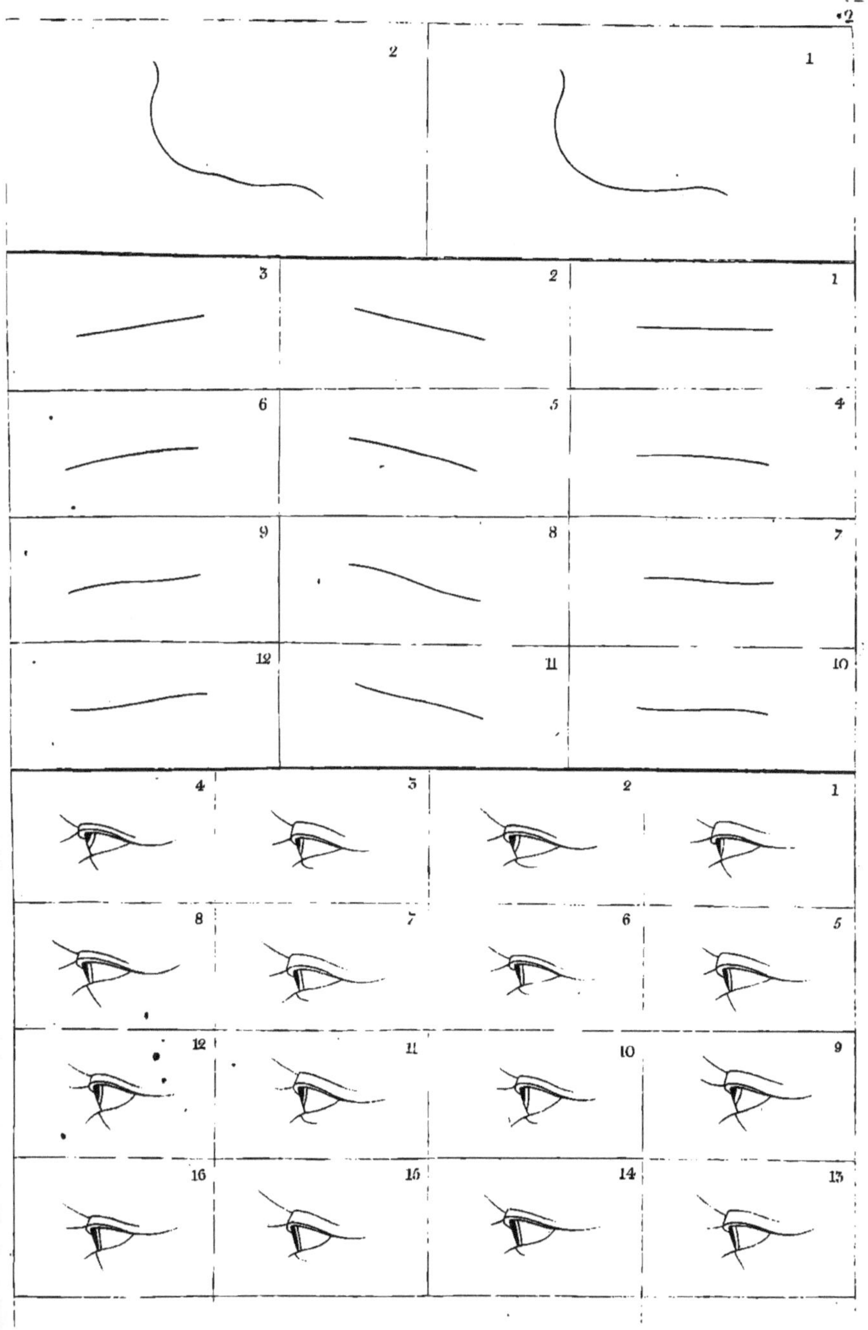

A. Cozens inv.

Publish'd April 10. 1777, by Alex.r Cozens, Leicester Street, Leicester Fields, London.

F. Bartolozzi sculp.

The Sensible, or wise. Beauté Spirituelle.

Alex^r. Cozens inv^t. Publish'd April 10. 1777, by Alex^r. Cozens Leicester Street, Leicester Fields, London. F. Bartolozzi sculp.

The Steady. *Beauté Determinée*

Publish'd April 10. 1777, by Alex.r Cozens, Leicester Street, Leicester Fields, London.

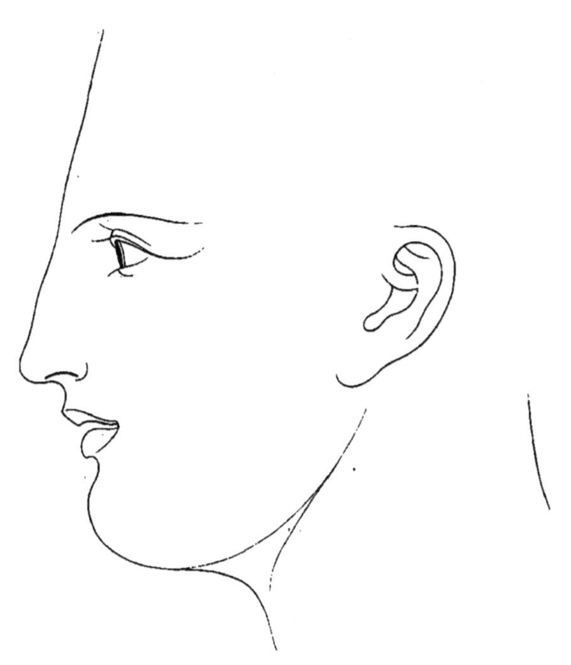

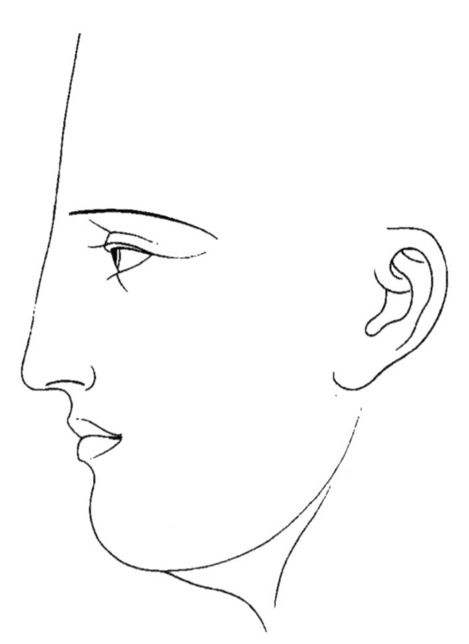

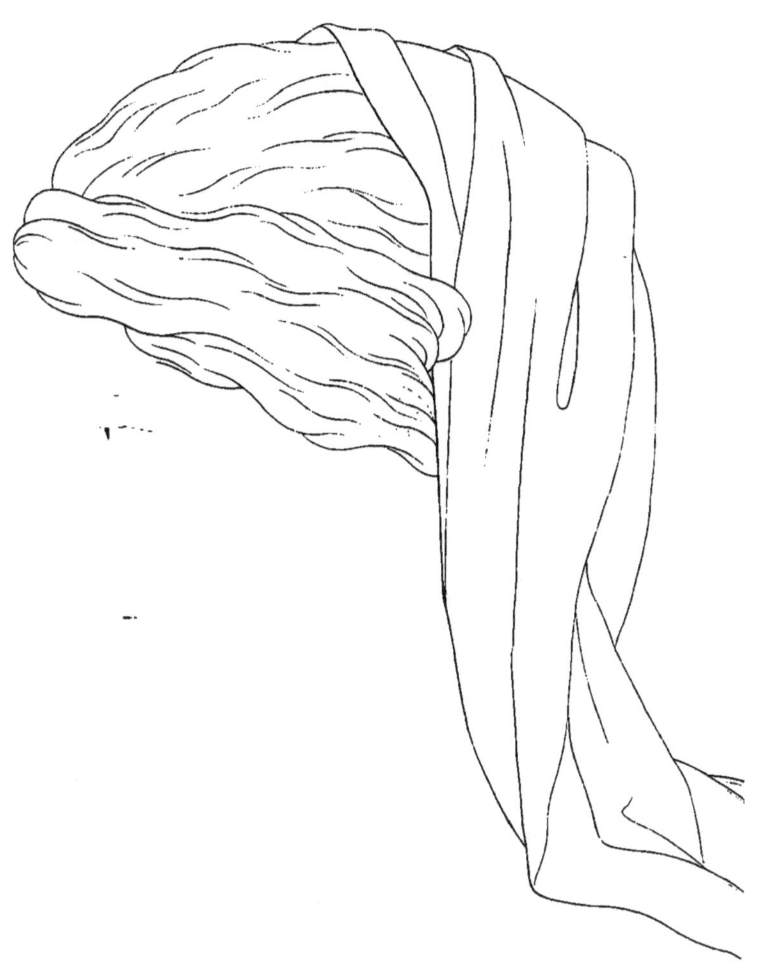

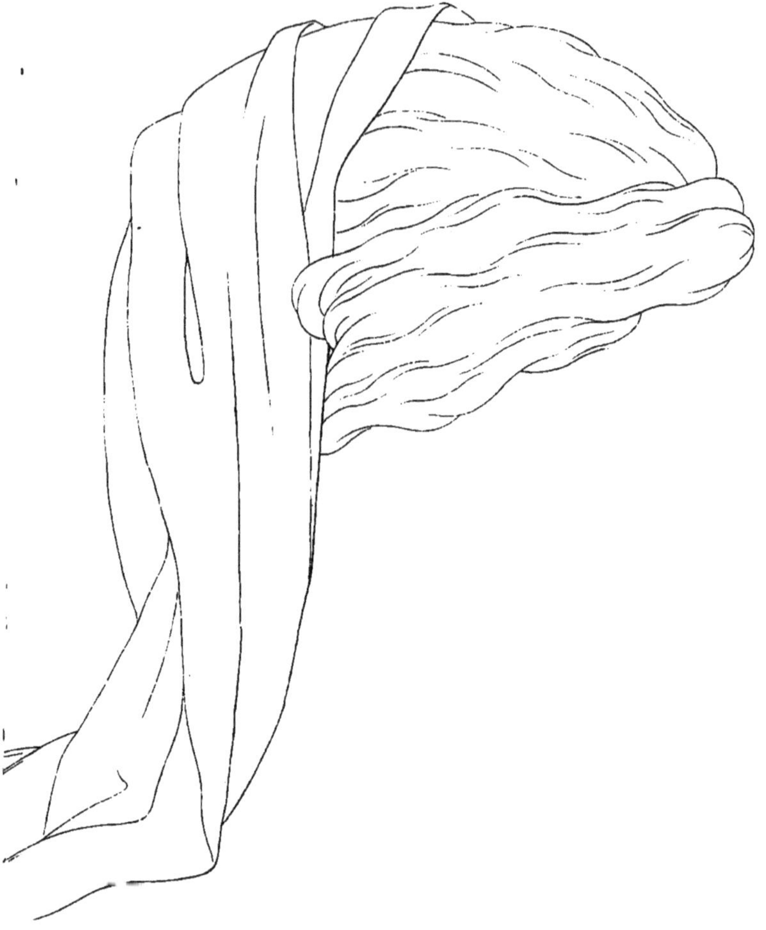

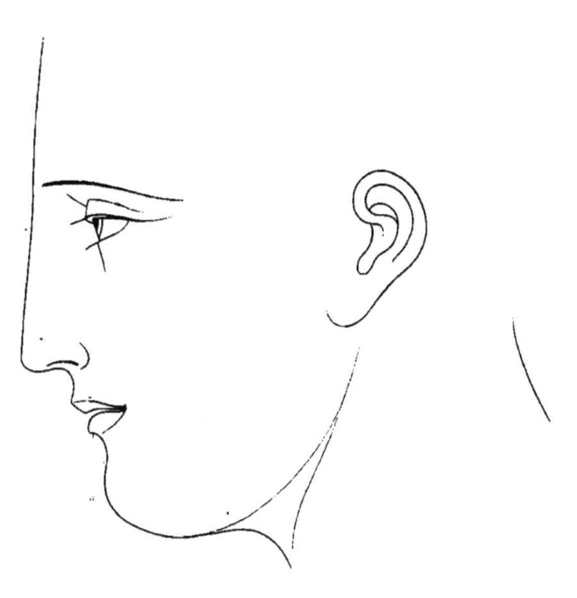

8.

F. Bartolozzi sculp.

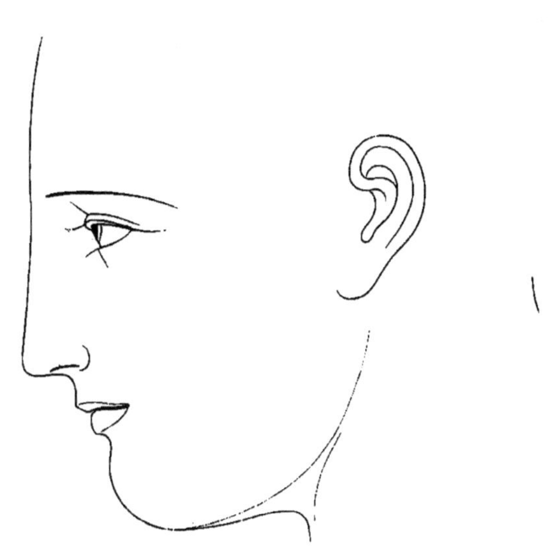

10

10

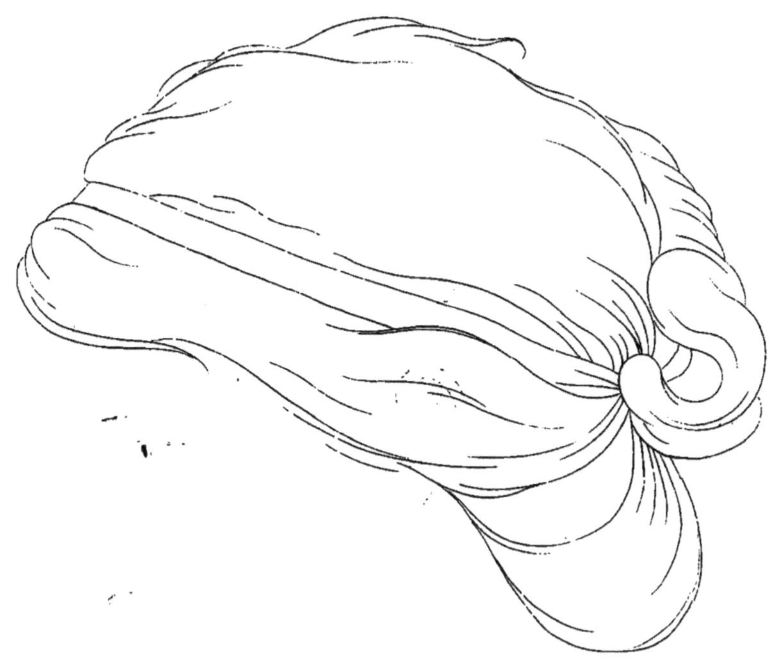

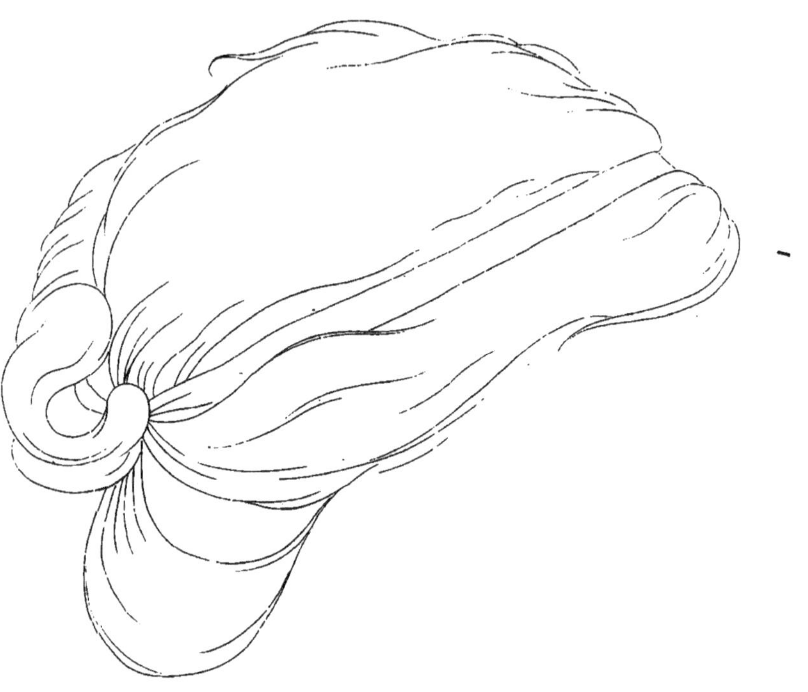

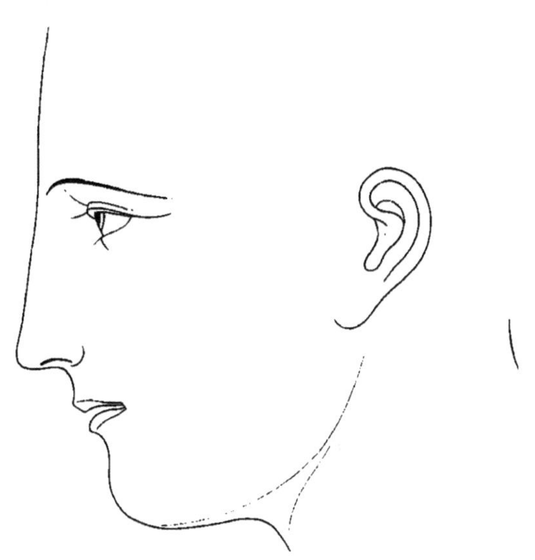

11

11

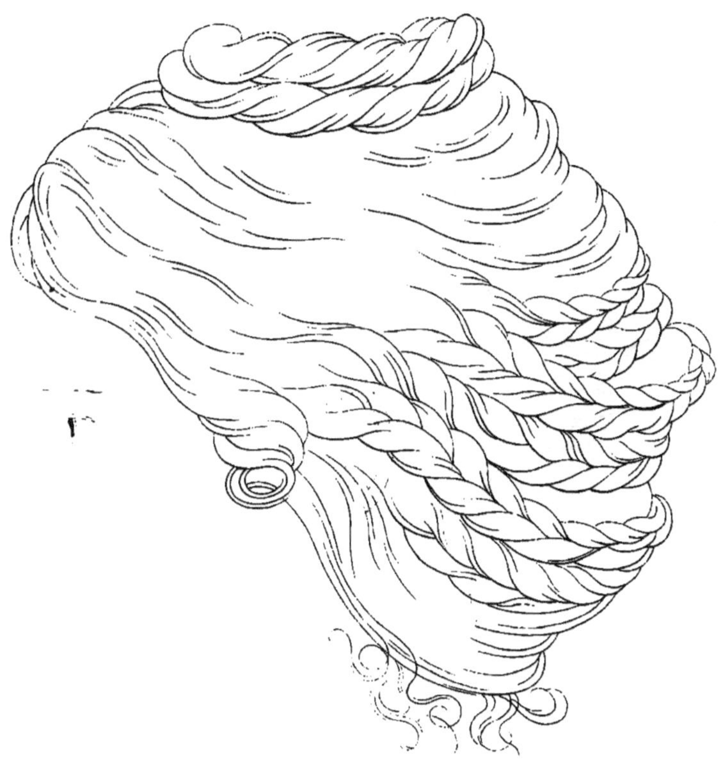

F. Bartolozzi sculp.

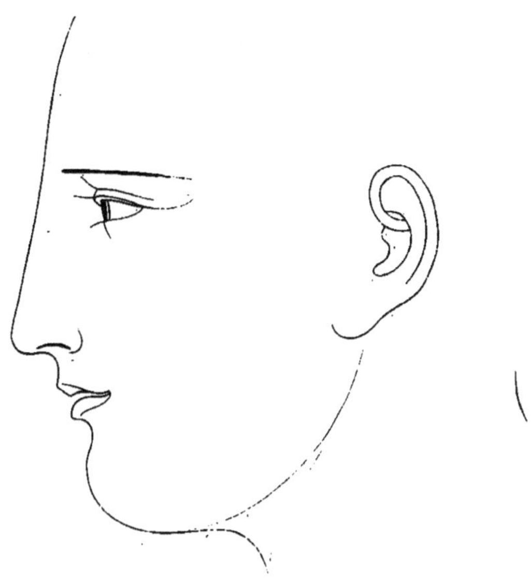

The Penetrating. *Beauté Intelligente*

Publish'd April 10. 1777, by Alex.r Cozens Leicester Street, Leicester Fields, London.

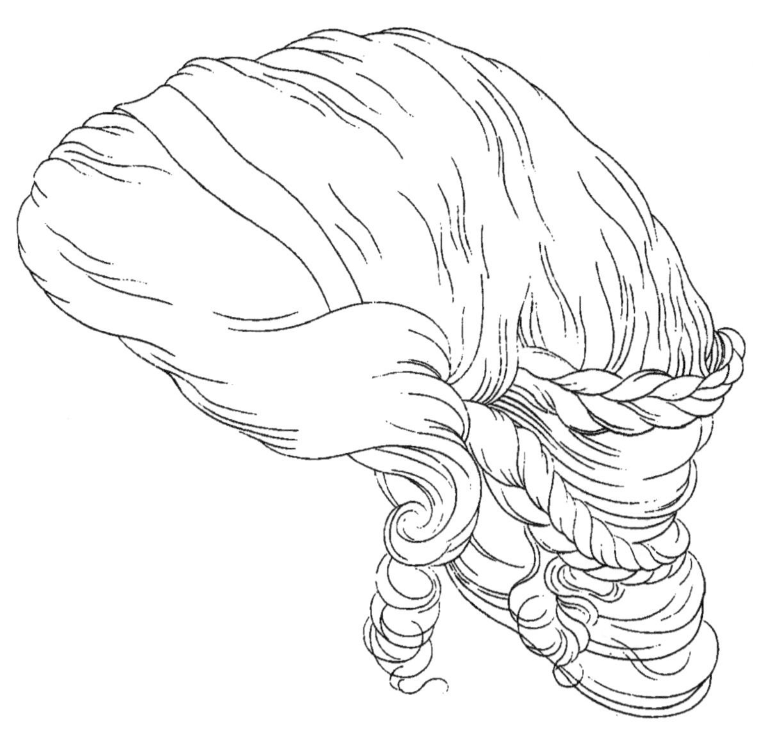

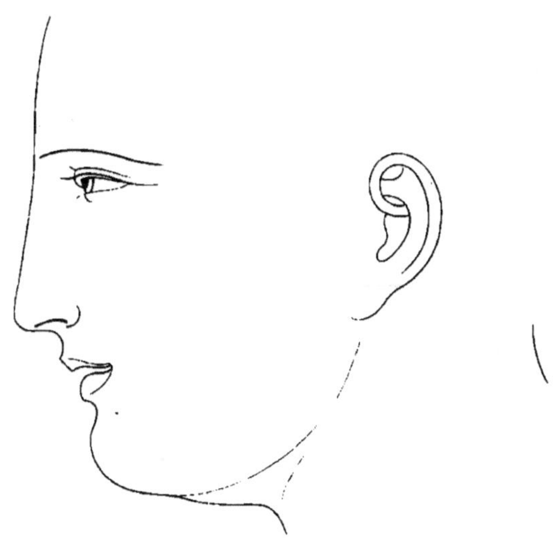

The Engaging.　　*Beauté prevenante.*

Publish'd April 10. 1777. by Alex.r Cozens, Leicester Street, Leicester Fields, London.

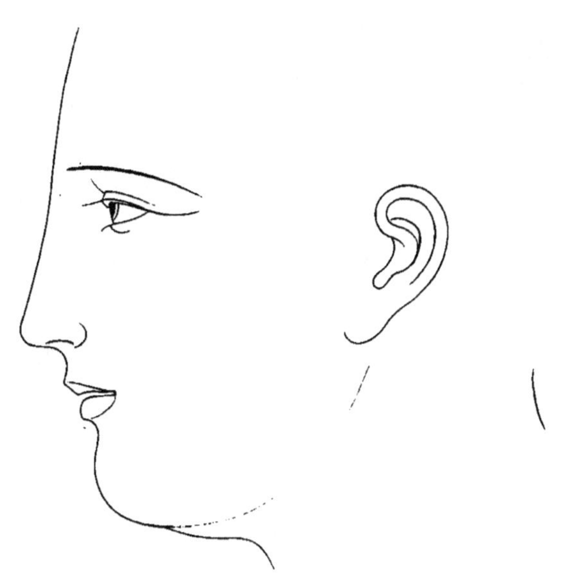

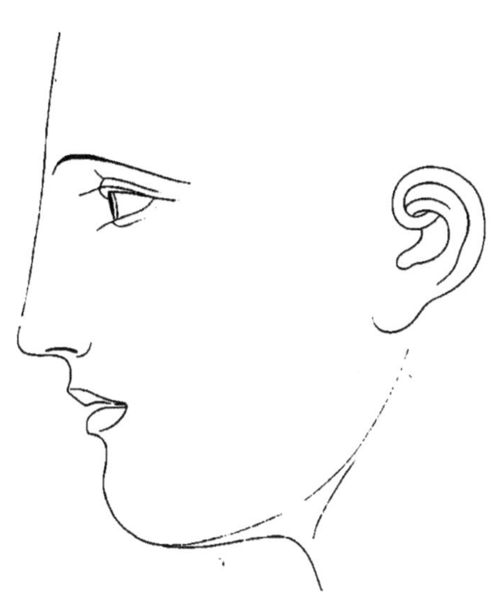

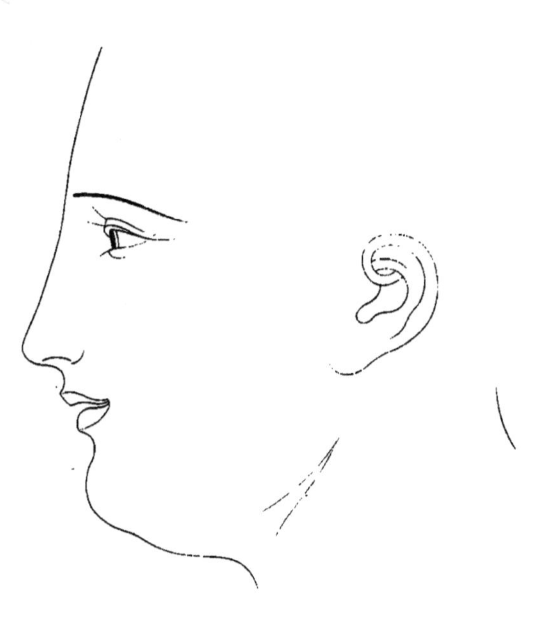

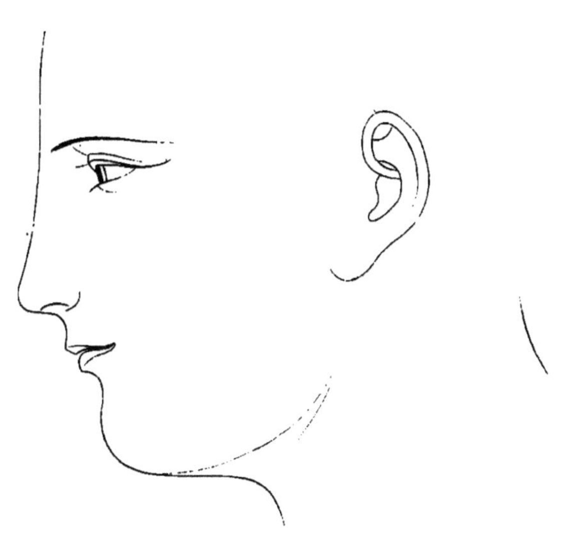

17

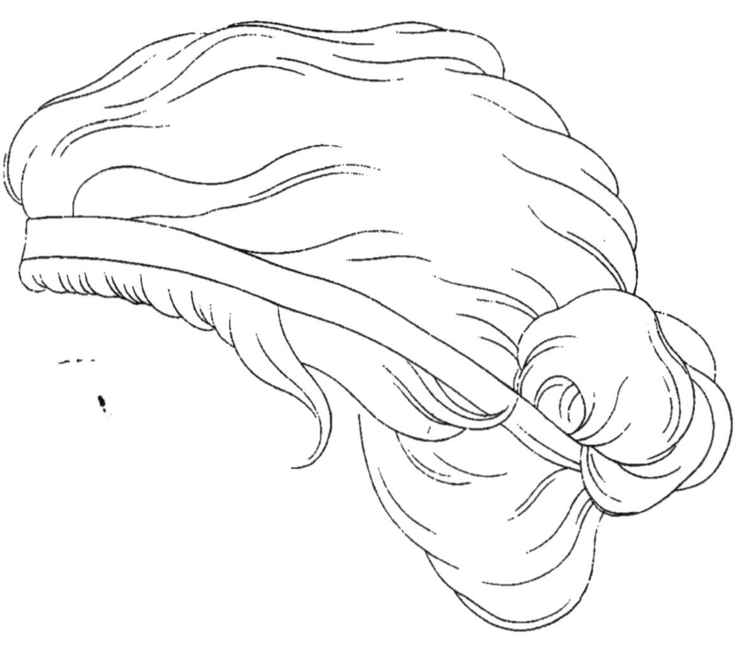

www.ingramcontent.com/pod-product-compliance
Lightning Source LLC
Chambersburg PA
CBHW030544270326
41927CB00008B/1503

* 9 7 8 3 3 3 7 3 1 0 9 6 7 *